The Creator's Plan and Pertinence

PRECEPTS AWAKENING OUR END-TIME VISION

T. F. Igler

NEW HARBOR PRESS

RAPID CITY, SD

Igler/New Harbor Press
1601 Mt Rushmore Rd, Ste 3288
Rapid City, SD 57701
www.NewHarborPress.com

Ordering Information:
Quantity sales. Special discounts are available on quantity purchases by corporations, associations, and others. For details, contact the "Special Sales Department" at the address above.

The Creator's Plan and Pertinence / Thomas Igler. -- 1st ed.
ISBN 978-1-63357-258-4

Contents

Preface

GOD'S *"WORD"* AND *"INTENT"*[1] are heavenly in origin. We are privileged to search out the often-veiled knowledge of godly precepts. Seeking the *"hidden wisdom"* (King James Version, 1 Corinthians 2:7), must be seasoned with the humble confession that divine orders proceed from the Creator's inner sanctum. The gift of knowledge pertaining to origins and purpose is proprietorial and occasioned only by God's predetermination. As per Jesus' statement, *"No man can come to me, except the Father which hath sent me draw him"* (John 6:44). God's grace in drawing us is ongoing and does not pertain solely to the conversion event. That being the case, there is no danger of an eventual spiritual exhaustion and discouragement as we progress away from worldliness. Lacking the continuing administering of grace, and an affinity to God's plan, would be equivalent to *"ever learning, and never able to come to the knowledge of the truth"* (2 Timothy 3:7). That is the earmark of an errant spiritual pursuit; forever circling the mountain instead of striking out for the Promised Land. Contrariwise, *"rightly dividing the word of truth"* equates to optimizing our walk with the Lord. To wit: Higher ground.

The Holy Spirit permits, even facilitates, interpretation and expounding of an inspired kind. In light of things allowed, the apostle Paul stated, *"I speak this by permission, and not of commandment"* (1 Corinthians 6:7). This passage treats a matter of human nature and the discourse does not nearly approach the immediacy of God's presence. On the other end of the spectrum, the context is very different when he states in 2 Corinthians 12:4, *"How that he was caught up into paradise, and heard unspeakable words, which it is not lawful for a man to utter."* Here, he introduces what can be termed the "ineffability factor." In the betwixt-and-between, there is an arena of properly acquiring and lawfully sharing of spiritual truths.

Prerequisite to an embrace of God's plan is that his chosen ones move away from a pride-driven mentality. What needs to be expressed here is that this subscription does not serve the creature. God's gift of truth serves most effectually in moving us to fear God, *"Stand in awe, and sin not."* There is no place in this forum for the self-serving. What pleases our Lord is humility, sacrifice, and loving him wholly. This book proceeds with that foundation of rightfully fearing, standing in awe, and loving the Creator. We are certain that he

---

1. In the volume of the book: KJV. Scripture in italics. Quotes are often without a reference. Added emphases throughout. The many repetitions are intentional. When helpful, part of a whole text may be repeated.

has allowed us to be party to his extraordinary plan of the *"restitution of all things."* Our favored position in the matter is *"that we might be the righteousness of God in him"* (2 Corinthians 5:21). Only therein can we stand justified as gratefully receiving and embracing his revealed omniscience and omnipotence. We know and we declare that, *"Thou art worthy, O Lord, to receive glory and honour and power: for thou hast created all things, and for thy pleasure they are and were created"* (Revelation 4:11).

The book of Jude is taken by "certain" of this generation, to be expressive of our present world, with a message in particular to the latter church. Verse 3 states, *"It was needful for me to write unto you, and exhort you that you should earnestly contend for the faith which was once delivered unto the saints."* The same "certain" take the liberty to teach that the *"faith"* includes the greater landscape of our "vision" and the embrace of God's plan. To that, I will not disagree. The *"earnestly contend"* should never be understood as contesting, incivility, or a mean-spirited stance. The *"earnestly contend,"* amongst the ecclesia, should be to *"earnestly contend"* against sin and unbelief. And so be it with this book and its author.

As the reader thoughtfully progresses in the reading of this book, they will become aware that many doctrinal settlements are questioned, even redefined. Again, there is no intention of getting into the arena of contest and distain. The greater fear of God and dread is the possibility that the Christian faith and hope would be discouraged. That would be counterproductive to our best intentions. This expositor desires to inform and clarify, so that God's plan will be better embraced, loved, and sought for.

Truth must be properly reported, and that is only possible if there is good basis toward our loving, merciful, and kind God. Then, as per God's generosity, we are given license to proceed.

Introduction

"*IN THE BEGINNING WAS the Word, and the Word was with God, and the Word was God*" (John 1:1). The English term *"Word,"* in the native idiom, is *"logos,"* and that reflects the idea of *"intent"* and determination. The correct treatment of this passage sets forth a foundational step toward understanding God's plan. Jesus Christ was the *"Word"* and he was *"even the mystery which hath been hid from ages and from generations, but now is made manifest to his saints"* (Colossians 1:26). Christ was from the beginning, and he was *"with God."* At the time prescribed, he was made manifest in the flesh (John 1:14). In Romans 1:4, the apostle Paul states that Christ was glorified and ascended to heaven as celestial and immortal, eternally by the Father's right hand. His Divinity is beyond question. Jesus proceeded from the Eternal Father, so He was "from the beginning." It is the Eternal God, even *"God, who quickeneth the dead, and calleth those things which be not as though they were"* (Romans 4:17). Genesis declares that there was *"light"* the first day and the light was good. It was the fourth day that the point of the emanation, or source, was revealed. A fitting similitude.

The heavenly *"innumerable company of angels"* themselves creative, were in perfect harmony with God's creative desires. To wit, God; *"above all,"* and sovereign, whose will and intent determined every detail of creation and the forthcoming human saga. God is the author of "unity." God is the author of "fruitful." God is the author of "order." An obedient Heavenly Host progressed wonderfully, being unified in their assignments and contributions toward the creation.

The crowning glory of the Creator and Heavenly Host: *"Let us make man in our image, after our likeness"* (Genesis 1:26). That "glory" equates to mankind's call to be family of God. *"Heirs of God, and joint-heirs with Christ"* (Romans 8:17). "Family" is the essence of this writing.

Great contest arises over the issue of literal versus symbolic "days" of creation. The whole issue pales when we believe and subordinate to the fact, with ramifications, that the Almighty God dwells in the Spirit realm. The creation could well have been accomplished in that realm and encompassed eons; and that with typical physical metamorphisms. Consider: Jesus transitioned from Spirit realm to the physical realm effortlessly. The disciples saw and believed. The high priest of theoretical physics and mathematics cannot begin to expound on the mechanics of that phenomenon. God occupies dimensions even beyond "time" and otherwise, beyond our capacity to entertain. To wit: God could have spoken his creation into our parameters; and he could have done it in literal days. The point being: Faith believing and humble confession negates many foolish arguments. Possibly that is akin to Paul's message when he said to Timothy, *"avoiding profane and vain babblings, and oppositions of science falsely so called: Which some professing have erred concerning the faith"* (1 Timothy 6:20, 21).

The Creator's Plan is *"the mother of us all."* He wills that we pursue His Plan, His *"Word,"* and *"intent,"* to the end of overturning the errant course man initiated. God's better prescription is that all of mankind finish the course of overcoming unto perfection. The end product is a new heaven and a new earth, where the perfected, *"finished,"* citizens abide as Holiness unto the Lord. This book purposes to endeavor in that arena of discussion.

CHAPTER 1

God's Plan Cannot Be Denied or Gotten Around

Question: What Are Those "Two Immutable Things" (Hebrews 6:18)?

THE BIBLE IS MULTIFACETED and layered. One insight reveals another layer of precepts, and then another. Isaiah 28:10 states, *"For precept must be upon precept, precept upon precept; line upon line, line upon line; here a little, and there a little."*

An answer to the above question, subheading, embarks toward the revelation of things hidden and precious. Beyond natural understanding, there is spiritual insight. *"For the Spirit searcheth all things, yea, the deep things of God"* (1 Corinthians 2:10). At times, in Holy Spirit communion, our inner man reaches toward that inner sanctum. Again, we mention the apostle Paul's reference in 2 Corinthians 12:4; *"How that he was caught up into paradise, and heard unspeakable words, which it is not lawful for a man to utter."* Every born-again child of God has the right to entertain and embrace life-changing Holy Ghost experiences. The five wise virgins, Matthew 25, had a reserve of knowledge. We need to understand that beyond "knowing," their lives were flavored with obedience. That gained them "experiential knowledge," and that is light. Those five were not only *"hearer,"* but *"doer of the work"* (James 1:25).

Hebrews 6:13–20. *"For when God made **promise** to Abraham, because he could swear by no greater, he sware by himself, 14. Saying, Surely blessing I will bless thee, and multiplying I will multiply thee. 15. And so, after he had patiently endured, he obtained **the promise**. 16. For men verily swear by the greater: and **an oath for confirmation** is to them an end of all strife. 17. Wherein God, willing more abundantly to shew unto the heirs of promise the **immutability of his counsel, confirmed it by an oath**: 18. That by **two immutable things,** in which it was impossible for God to lie, we might have a strong consolation, who have fled for refuge to lay hold upon the hope set before us: 19. Which hope we have as an anchor of the soul, both sure and steadfast, and which entereth into that within the veil; 20. Whither the forerunner is for us entered, even Jesus, made an high priest for ever after the order of Melchisedec."*

As per the above Scripture, it appears that the obvious answer is, first, the *"**promise.**"* Second or *"**confirmed,**"* was the *"**oath.**"* That answer might suffice, and it is correct. However, beyond this hearing, is an understanding that connects to the believer's estate of "faith-believing." That is an "in-Christ" estate, where we know, without a shadow of doubt that God's intent, with an oath, is upon us, **called**. We are first called according to his purpose and, second, we are sealed "in Christ" according to the Spirit of promise, **chosen**. Being chosen equates to being Children of God having place and *"members in particular."* New Testament terminology. Furthermore, we are obedient and faithful participants in the "Plan" and finalized with *"the restitution of all things"* (Acts 3:21).

We are increasing in our relationship, understanding, and in the wisdom of the Lord. Our searching prayerfully into God's word is ongoing; a work in progress. This brief writing might be regarded as a "draft." The more complete answer to the title question would be the "assurance" we have in this experiential walk "in Christ." Exalting God's plan for our lives is the aim of Paul's New Testament reiteration of the fact of "Promise and Oath." We see this initiation early on with Abraham. Abraham is the father of faith. We are his offspring, ourselves being children of faith. Faith and obedience give forth the experiential part. That is, a move from *"hearer"* to the blessed estate of *"doer."* Abraham was that first complete person; as we regard him, "Father of Faith."

Genesis 22:1–18 gives the narrative of Abraham offering Isaac. Isaac was the child of promise. The author of that promise required the death of that promise, in a sense, and Abraham was obedient. The thing pleased God. Genesis 22:16–18 states, *"And said, By myself have I sworn, saith the LORD, for because thou hast done this thing, and hast not withheld thy son, thine only son: 17. That in blessing I will bless thee, and in multiplying I will multiply thy seed as the stars of the heaven, and as the sand which is upon the sea shore; and thy seed shall possess the gate of his enemies; 18. And in thy seed shall all the nations of the earth be blessed, because thou hast obeyed my voice."*

Hebrews 11:19 states, *"Accounting that God was able to raise him up, even from the dead; from whence also he received him in a figure."*

In greater part, Abraham's obedience rested in his embrace, by faith, of the resurrecting power of God. From that trust and obedience, God gave forth the "oath." It was established. Again, it was the product of faith and obedience. The "oath" is that part where Abraham moved into "partnership" with God. He became part and party to God's plan. It relates to us in that it is the believer's duty to "do," being obedient, according to the promise. It is the gist of Romans 5:10, *"For if, when we were enemies, we were reconciled to God by the death of his Son, much more, being reconciled, we shall be saved by his* <u>*life*</u>*."* This Scripture shows us that going forward from "hearing" and embracing Christ's gift of reconciliation, we must "do" according to Jesus' example. The Oracle is Jesus Christ; his *life* because he fulfilled all things and he *"finished"* God's prophesied plan for his life on earth. Even so for us, going forward is to conform to the oath, being in league with and a "participant in the plan of God."

Hebrews 6:1 states; *"Therefore leaving the principles of the doctrine of Christ, let us go on unto perfection; not laying again the foundation of repentance from dead works, and of faith toward God."* This *"go on"* is noteworthy because it indicates that beyond "hearing" a thing, there is an establishing of that thing in our hearts by faith, which would be the "doing" of a thing . . . the "obedience" factor. That is the more complete understanding of the text in its broader context. Later in the book, it will be refreshed that "obedience" is accomplished as a matter of "loving God."

The Related Precepts and Similitudes

Genesis 14:18, 19—*"And Melchizedek king of Salem brought forth bread and wine: and he was the priest of the most high God. 19. And he blessed him, and said, Blessed be Abram of the most high God, possessor of heaven and earth."*

This Melchizedek is Christ, or, at least a reflection of Christ. Whoever the personage was, some say Shem, it was Christ's order, and the abovementioned statement of Hebrews 6:20 makes that clear. *"Jesus, made an high priest for ever after the order of Melchisedec."* Also, on the point in question of Christ very presence; consider that it is *"God, who quickeneth the dead, and <u>calleth those things which be not as though they were</u>"* (Romans 4:17).

Abram was blessed by Melchizedek shortly after a military victory. Following that blessing, Abram declined all rewards of men's offerings. Going forward to chapter 15, Abram has a vision.

Genesis 15:9–12—*"And he said unto him, Take me an heifer of three years old, and a she goat of three years old, and a ram of three years old, and a turtledove, and a young pigeon. 10. And he took unto him all these, and divided them in the midst, and laid each piece one against another: but the birds divided he not. 11. And when the fowls came down upon the carcasses, Abram drove them away. 12. And when the sun was going down, a deep sleep fell upon Abram; and, lo, an horror of great darkness fell upon him."*

Genesis 15:17–18—*"And it came to pass, that, when the sun went down, and it was dark, behold a <u>smoking furnace</u>, and a <u>burning lamp</u> that passed between those pieces. 18. In the same day the LORD made a covenant with Abram, saying, Unto thy seed have I given this land, from the river of Egypt unto the great river, the river Euphrates."*

This is a landmark covenant. The caricatures pertaining to the ritual probably include the idea of Abraham's seed enduring the <u>furnace of affliction</u> and experiencing <u>God's leading</u>, per Moses' leadership. It is known also, by Paul's spoken revelation, that Christ was present; not necessarily the individuality of Jesus, but personified as per the *"Rock."* 1 Corinthians 10:1, 4 states, *"Moreover, brethren, I would not that ye should be ignorant, how that all our fathers were under the cloud, and all passed through the sea . . . 4. And did all drink the same spiritual drink: for they drank of that spiritual Rock that followed them: and <u>that Rock was Christ</u>."*

Relating to Jesus being a party to the ritual of Genesis 15:9–17, see Revelation 1:14, 15. *"His head and his hairs were white like wool, as white as snow; and <u>his eyes were as a flame of fire</u>; 15. And his <u>feet like unto fine brass, as if they burned in a furnace</u>; and his voice as the sound of many waters."* Jesus was that divinity present in John's vision and in Abram's vision. To wit: If Jesus is the revealed plan of God and the plan is unaltered and irrefutable, as is God, then Christ is likewise. He was present *"in the midst of the seven candlesticks,"* and he was integral to every promise, oath, and covenant; and, so, he was in Abraham's encounter with Melchizedek.

Going forward: Strong's Concordance gives the definition of *immutable* as unchangeable. In the overview; God cannot be moved around and his determinations cannot be avoided or ignored. God told Moses, *"I AM*

THAT I AM: *and he said, Thus shalt thou say unto the children of Israel, I AM hath sent me unto you"* (Exodus 3:14). Moses had that connection, unity, and there was no overturning or reversal of that commission. God is the unity and the continuity of all things. That is the nature of his omniscience. Concerning Christ, Paul states in Hebrews 13:8, *"Jesus Christ the same yesterday, and today, and for ever."* That *"same,"* or sameness, is absolute, irrefutable, and immutable. The fact being Jesus was in unity, or oneness, with his Father. Scripture bears out that truth.

Hebrews 11:6 states, *"For he that cometh to God must believe that he is, and that he is a rewarder of them that diligently seek him."* Our calling is according to the promise and our being chosen is commensurate with our "doing," as obedient servants. Jesus said, *"For many are called, but few are chosen"* (Matthew 22:14).

In all the above references, there is the presence and flavor of divinity, continuance, and unity. A more perfect doctrine, correctly expressed, will better declare our faith. God's "chosen," by their confession and demeanor, manifest that these features are integral with the "NAME of JESUS." He is our resting place, our station, our consolation, our gift of God, and from God, even the Grace that we have "in Christ," so that, in Jesus we are in agreement, or oneness, with the Father. We do well to rest in the immutability of his promise and oath. We are blessed in our oneness with Christ and the Father's good intentions.

A word of encouragement: We are family. Be assured, the Lord desires that we embrace his blessings, promises, even being at one with him in the revelation of the oath. *"For the testimony of Jesus is the spirit of Prophecy"* (Revelation 19:10). As Jesus stated the prophesied blessing: *"In my Father's house* (household) *are many mansions* (new bodies with sonship) *if it were not so, I would have told you, I go to prepare a place for you"* (John 14:2).

The God and Father of our Lord and Savior Jesus and His Christ desires that we be perfected in our faith and the Promise and the performance of the Oath. That is what and why he said, *"Wherein God, willing more abundantly to shew unto the heirs of promise the immutability of his counsel, confirmed it by an oath: 18. That by two immutable things, in which it was impossible for God to lie, we might have a strong consolation."* Again, Hebrews 6:17, 18.

We have taken care not to add to or take away from the truth. This correct and honorable treatment of searching out the matter touches God's omnipotence and God's omniscience.

Note: You may think it would be impossible to overly embellish these features of God, but there may be a dreadful subtlety present. To wit: When we wax eloquent on the matter of God's greatness, a prideful aspect may enter our limited mentality: The exaltation of thinking that we have somehow concluded the matter, or even entertain the misconception that we can "qualify" God's omniscience. In which case, a subtle transfer sometimes occurs where our glorifying God moves over to glorifying self, even exalting ourselves. When and if that happens, it translates into a mean and belittling attitude that reflects disdainfully on others, at least, others who disagree with our exalted manner of exalting God. Pray it not be so. That would be a mean-spirited judgeship that issues death sentences or banishments; a *"putting away"* spirit which God hates (Malachi 2:16). That would be the most dreaded estate of a flawed Christian endeavor. Again, pray it not be so. Sadly, history does declare those excesses.

We confess God's demonstrated omniscience and omnipotence in bringing his plan to fruition, and that with infinite detail.

God gives his disciples no "chair" accommodating personal acclaim. Such being our humble estate, it seems fitting, early on, to bring to the record this required contrition.

CHAPTER 2

Creation, Garden of Eden, Sin, and Redemption

Treating Basic Parameters, the "Fall," Judgment, and Restitution

THIS SECTION MIGHT BE termed the "overview." It begins with the principals present in the Garden of Eden. We are particularly interested in the two trees, the fruits of the trees, and the serpent. A true perception of these five principals, with ramifications, will benefit a foundational understanding of God's plan. Thus, we will be helped in gaining that insightful understanding of the present truth. The truth that includes our oneness with Christ in *"the sure mercies of David"* (Acts 13:34). Going forward, the discussion concludes when God's plan is fully accomplished.

Let it be humbly stated that only by the Lord's grace can we confess to the understanding of God's plan for *"the times of restitution of all things"* (Acts 3:21). Beyond knowing, there is the blessed estate of partnership in the fulfilling of God's plan. Man's part in the partnership is held, as simultaneous, with both great trepidation and great assurance. Unity with God's will is a sure resting place. The apostle Paul is very pastoral in his concern when he states, *"Let us therefore fear, lest, a promise being left us of entering into his rest, any of you should seem to come short of it"* (Hebrews 4:1).

Necessarily, several related issues and thoughts are brought forth and discussed. The time and space given to the discussion is generous. The whole of the matter pertains to the plan, *"which is the mother of us all"* (Galatians 4:26).

Genesis 1

Genesis 1:1, 2—1. *"In the beginning God created the heaven and the earth. 2. And the earth was without form and void; and darkness was upon the face of the deep. And the Spirit of God moved upon the face of the waters."*

Question and discussion begin early with these first verses of the Bible. Was there an earlier, populated, civilized earth, predating Adam? Was it destroyed and rendered *"without form and void?"* With many students, this particular issue is off the table. The reason being, it predates the starting point of the Bible narrative. It has been said; you can go there (a pre-Bible supposed narrative), but you are on your own. Notwithstanding, serious discussions persist on that point. Adherents reject the idea that a pre-Adamic world is a speculative or an out-of-line issue. True believers are convinced their concepts and resulting additions to God's plan of the earth's restoration and man's salvation are thoughtful and significant. It is not within the scope of this article to delve into the exegetical and contextual studies involved. The possibility of a pre-Adamic world, with ramifications, should be treated carefully and with some regard.

The writer does not reject the idea of a pre-Adamic world. However, there is good reason to consider the matter of "ineffability" relating to an in-depth study of this issue. The discussion would carry forward to the idea that there was "contest in the heavens." That is, obedience and disobedience in the angelic ranks. That matter is not explicitly mentioned in the Genesis text. Again, it may constitute a realm of involvement that is God's business, presently transcending man's need to know. Even so, there may be a grudging agreement that mere study, consideration, and confession would suffice. That is, a pursuit denying going forward to establish the hypothesis in the hearts or spirits of others.

As somewhat justifying further discussion, this preexistence issue relates directly to another subject that some ministers do consider vital, current, and presently in man's arena of a need-to-know. To wit: If there is a fallen angel, Satan, an individuality opposing God, then does his origin likewise predate creation's story and mankind's story as it was given to us? That is a valid question and it may validate a need-to-know. The devil argument, excuse the expression, cannot be settled satisfactorily without some consideration of "origin." Blind spots accepted, a spirited contest continues on this subject. The argument seems to settle out as literalizing versus spiritualizing the Scripture. As per our terminology, *literal* tends to substantiate a literal individuality-Devil viewpoint and *spiritualizing* tends to symbolize the Devil as evil, merely emblematic, and not as individuality. Even those definitions can be argued.

Now the question arises: Does the devil issue likewise have an "ineffability" consideration? This question goes close to the heart of the purpose of this writing. We can only answer by saying, "If there is not a principle need-to-know, or if approaching a subject is premature, we must ask: 'Lord, what do you think of that subject?'" First, is the nature of the battle beyond our playing field? Or, second, is it a matter of a right-to-know, but not a right-to-engage? On the more acceptable side, we might choose the latter. Jude 9 reads, *"Yet Michael the archangel, when contending with the devil he disputed about the body of Moses, durst not bring against him a railing accusation, but said, The Lord rebuke thee."* Michael's holdback was not a lack of power or authority; rather, it centered on the matter of justification with respect to the future advent of the cross, and that price paid being the eventual settlement of the contest. It is more a matter of time and season. While no person compares himself to Michael, we do consider the comparable having to do with justification, as per the New Testament message.

This paper proceeds with an awareness that we should not require faith-believing in areas of conjecture, or even truth, when it is an out-of-order or out-of-season endeavor. Also, there is the possibility that God does not want certain areas of understanding to become a sort of earmark of His Body. If God wanted us to settle onto a foundation of faith-believing in pre-Bible suppositions, or other, then, would he not have spelled it out clearly and unmistakably? After all, *"We both labor and suffer reproach, because we trust in the living God"* (1 Timothy 4:10). With evil, we have no such like suffering, affinity, or trust, pre-Adamic or present.

At best, some contest may provide a testing as to our love toward the whole brotherhood, and at worst a source of division. Again, there is a difference in reasonably knowing something, versus embracing a thing by faith. A valid concern is that we might follow our desire of greater faith with the hope of some experiential event. No Christian should solicit an experience with anything evil for the purpose of furthering their belief system.

Concerning things unseen, we have need of faith. Our love for the brotherhood should lead us away from experiences or faith-believing in the arena of evil establishments.

Genesis 1:3—*"And God said, Let there be light: and there was light."*

Light in this passage, as per the Hebrew definition, gives the first interpretation as being "illumination." That would not necessarily designate a point of emanation, but states that the earth was lighted.

Genesis 1:4, 5—4. *"And God saw the light, that it was good: and God divided the light from the darkness."* 5. And God called the light Day, and the darkness he called Night. And the evening and the morning were the <u>first day</u>."

From the onset, God, in a literal sense, intended to make a difference in light and darkness, and that the light was good. Scripture reflects on the separation issue throughout. *"Divided the light from the darkness"* is a profound similitude as it is set forth in the Scripture. Sanctification is good. Again, from the onset, light is good.

Genesis 1:6–8—6. *"And God said, Let there be a firmament in the midst of the waters, and let it divide the waters from the waters. 7. And God made the firmament, and divided the waters which were under the firmament from the waters which were above the firmament: and it was so. 8. And God called the firmament Heaven. And the evening and the morning were the* <u>second day</u>.*"*

The result of the second day of creation was *"Heaven."* It was the space and basic provision for the land, which would be a third day event.

Genesis 1:9–13—9. *"And God said, Let the waters under the heaven be gathered together unto one place, and let the dry land appear: and it was so. 10. And God called the dry land Earth; and the gathering together of the waters called he Seas: and God saw that it was good. 11. And God said, Let the earth bring forth grass, the herb yielding seed, and the fruit tree yielding fruit after his kind, whose seed is in itself, upon the earth: and it was so. 12. And the earth brought forth grass, and herb yielding fruit, whose seed was in itself, after his kind: and God saw that it was good. 13. And the evening and the morning were the* <u>third day</u>.*"*

God's provision: It was to be man's abiding place, a habitable physical realm. The firmament, as set forth on day two, was a heaven without provision for land animals. On this third day, we have the *"dry land Earth"* and the *"Seas,"* capable of giving all living things a source of sustenance.

Genesis 1:14–19—14. *"And God said, Let there be lights in the firmament of the heaven to divide the day from the night; and let them be for signs, and for seasons, and for days, and years: 15. And let them be for lights in the firmament of the heaven to give light upon the earth: and it was so. 16. And God made two great lights; the greater light to rule the day, and the lesser light to rule the night: he made the stars also. 17. And God set them in the firmament of the heaven to give light upon the earth, 18. And to rule over the day and over the night, and to divide the light from the darkness: and God saw that it was good. 19. And the evening and the morning were the* <u>fourth day</u>.*"*

It is understood that God is referring to the sun and the moon when he said, *"Let there be lights,"* and when he said he *"made two great lights."* The Hebrew language definition refers to the sun and moon as a luminous body or luminary. As such, the first day of creation didn't indicate a "point of emanation" for the light. Here, day four, the sun and the moon are points, or observable sources of the light. As per similitude, it was in the fourth thousand years that Christ came, when God, the Light and the Life, was revealed thru Jesus Christ.

The lights, the sun and the moon, are spoken of as in the firmament or seemingly within the firmament. Obviously, the sun and moon are beyond our habitation (atmosphere). They are "observed" as being within our firmament or heaven.

Genesis 1:20–23—20. *"And God said, Let the waters bring forth abundantly the moving creature that hath life, and the fowl that may fly above the earth in the open firmament of heaven. 21 And God created great whales, and every living creature that moveth, which the waters brought forth abundantly, after their kind, and every winged fowl after his kind: and God saw that it was good. 22. And God blessed them, saying, Be fruitful, and multiply, and fill the waters in the seas, and let fowl multiply in the earth. 23. And the evening and the morning were the* <u>fifth day</u>.*"*

Note: The Evolutionist could make declarations regarding these verses. Their position would be to see the waters as the source of life and the fowls as evolving from the sea. Their position is very strong in nomenclature as well as fossil remains interpreted as proofs; impressive in that regard. Pity the man that undertakes to seriously contend with them. Rarely will he prevail in changing minds; the nomenclature being overwhelming, and, if that be flavored with the pride factor, you might count the contest counterproductive at best. We would rather make simply understood declarations and statements as proof, showing God's unlimited greatness as per the multitudes of variety, size, and beauty of both fishes and fowls. We are also inclined to cite as proof an ecological balance and design that defies chance.

Genesis 1:24, 25—24. *"And God said, Let the earth bring forth the living creature after his kind, cattle, and creeping thing, and beast of the earth after his kind: and it was so. 25. And God made the beast of the earth after his kind, and cattle after their kind, and every thing that creepeth upon the earth after his kind: and God saw that it was good."*

Now, the earth brings forth. That is a brief and concise statement. We know that God created, as per sea and air, a multitude of living creatures. *"After his kind"* and *"after their kind"* are repeated five times in total. There would be no cross mixing of the species.

Genesis 1:26–28—26. *"And God said, Let us make man* <u>in our image</u>, *after* <u>our</u> <u>likeness</u>: *and let them have* <u>dominion</u> *over the fish of the sea, and over the fowl of the air, and over the cattle, and over all the earth, and over every creeping thing that creepeth upon the earth. 27. So God created man* <u>in his own image</u>, <u>in the image of God</u> *created he him; male and female created he them. 28. And God blessed them, and God said unto them, Be* <u>fruitful</u>, *and* <u>multiply</u>, *and* <u>replenish</u> *the earth, and* <u>subdue it</u>*: and have* <u>dominion</u> *over the fish of the sea, and over the fowl of the air, and over every living thing that moveth upon the earth."*

Note: The statements, *"In our image, our likeness: . . . in his own image, in the image of God"* are repeated for clarity and emphasis. The statement of *"dominion"* is also repeated for emphasis. Man, in his pre-sin state of innocence, was endowed with <u>dominion</u> over all creation, <u>communion</u> with God, and an unaltered <u>con-science</u> toward God's will. These are spiritual attributes, and no other creature has these "likenesses" and "connections" to God. These are *"the image of God"* features of mankind. These verses, 26–28, expressed God's original intent for mankind.

Psalms 8:6—*"Thou madest him to have dominion over the works of thy hands; thou hast put all things under his feet:"* This passage is a restatement of this <u>dominion</u>, but it concludes, at that point, in the second man, Adam; Christ and his house. While this original statement in Genesis did pertain to the first man Adam, the fulfilling of God's intent will be realized in Jesus Christ and his household of born-again, overcomer-status, believers.

Romans 8:14 states, *"For as many as are* <u>led</u> *by the Spirit of God, they are the sons of God."* This New Testament Scripture relates to *"*<u>dominion</u>*"* as it was originally given Adam. However, now it refers to an intuitive know-ing and, thus, leading. The leading is of the Holy Ghost, and directs us to depart from evil. So that: Presently, dominion relates more to power over a sinful nature than to any domination over the natural habitat. As we term it, dominion over the "old man."

Genesis 1:29, 30—29. *"And God said, Behold, I have given you every herb bearing seed, which is upon the face of all the earth, and every tree, in the which is the fruit of a tree yielding seed; to you it shall be for meat. 30. And to every beast of the earth, and to every fowl of the air, and to every thing that creepeth upon the earth, wherein there is life, I have given every green herb for meat: and it was so."*

God bestows to man, beast, fowl, and creeping things, the right and blessing of natural sustenance, as provided by his hand, by way of the herbs and trees of the earth. No mention is made of eating flesh.

Genesis 1:31—*"And God saw every thing that he made, and, behold, it was very good. And the evening and the morn-ing were the* <u>sixth day</u>*."*

This statement was all-encompassing and the creation altogether pleasing, as God viewed his six day's work. Thus far, there were only "dos": *"Be fruitful, and multiply, and replenish the earth, and subdue it: and have dominion"* (Genesis 1:28).

Genesis 2

Genesis 2:1–3—*1. "Thus the heavens and the earth were finished, and all the host of them. 2. And on* <u>the seventh day God ended his work which he had made</u>*; and he rested on the seventh day from all his work which he had made.*

3. And God blessed the seventh day, and sanctified it: because that in it he had rested from all his work which God created and made."

It is obvious that God put the seventh day into a special category. *"Sanctified"* is a high station. The Jews of Jesus' time likewise revered the Sabbath and counted it as sanctified. Also, they considered the creation as resting with them and that God had indeed rested it with them. Jesus made this comment on the Sabbath day, *"My father worketh hitherto, and I work"* (John 5:17). The Jews tried to kill him, and that was a reasonable reaction, from their standpoint. God initially rested the creation with Adam and they felt they had that same post with God. Jesus cut right across their pride of being the keepers of God's rest. In the continued story of Adam, we see that he failed, as did the Jews of Christ's day. (The New Testament narrative doesn't indicate the Jews actually perceived that fact as the underlying reason for their wrathful reactions to Jesus' statement.)

Genesis 2:4–7—4. *"These are the generations of the heavens and of the earth when they were created, in the day that the Lord God made the earth and the heavens, 5. And every plant of the field before it was in the earth, and every herb of the field before it grew: for the Lord God had not caused it to rain upon the earth, and there was not a man to till the ground. 6. But there went up a mist from the earth, and watered the whole face of the ground. 7. And the Lord God formed man of the dust of the ground, and breathed into his nostrils the breath of life; and man became a living soul."*

We now ask the question. Was the creation six literal twenty-four-hour days? Specific thoughts and questions regarding a day and the time consideration may be a moot subject. Verse 4 states, *"The generations of the heavens and of the earth when they were created, in the day that the Lord God made the earth and the heavens."* Here, a *day* refers to the time of the creation, or, as per Strong's, figuratively, a space of time defined by an associated term. The report is given as *"the evening and the morning"* indicating literal days. Moot question or not, the possibility of six literal twenty-four-hour days remains. This matter was alluded to in the third paragraph of the Introduction and refreshed here. To wit:

With God all things are possible. God's habitation is the Spirit realm. But does he create to-be-material things in the Spirit realm? Confessedly, we have no way of knowing that, nor the time dimensions, nor the mechanics of the realm of the Spirit. We confess that God could have created in a no-time realm and spoken the creation into existence. That is, spoken creation from a Spirit realm into the material, physical realm. We, thus, confess to the possibility of literal twenty-four-hour days. Jesus demonstrated an effortless transitioning from Spirit realm to material realm in his several appearances to his disciples after his glorification.

Verses 5 and 6—5. *"And every plant of the field <u>before it was in the earth</u>, and every herb of the field <u>before it grew</u>: for the Lord God had not caused it to rain upon the earth, and there was not a man to till the ground. 6. But there went up a mist from the earth, and watered the whole face of the ground."*

Verses 5 and 6 give us reason to think God started with the plant first and then the seed. The proverbial question: Which came first, the chicken or the egg? The chicken wins.

There was no man to till the ground, and no rain; just mist for watering. The atmosphere above remained aloft, in total. Relative to our present post-flood era, there was much more atmospheric protection from the rays of the sun and much higher atmospheric pressure. That meant more oxygen in the blood. Both are very advantageous for human and animal health. On that point, supposedly prehistoric, huge animal remains have been unearthed and some have been determined to have insufficient lung capacity. The flood resulted in a reduced atmospheric pressure, resulting in less oxygen transmitted to the blood. That would have spelled their demise. Obviously, the rain and Noah's flood were future to Adam's day. Mankind's life-span declined after the flood, and as well, we note the absence of those large animals.

Verse 7—*"And the Lord God formed man of the dust of the ground, and breathed into his nostrils the breath of life; and man became a living soul."*

This verse gives us the basic ingredients pertaining to spirit, soul, and body: From the dust, God formed a physical tabernacle (body). He breathed life (spirit) into that vessel and it became a living person (soul).

Genesis 2:8–17—8. *"And the Lord God planted a garden eastward in Eden; and there he put the man whom he had formed. 9. And out of the ground made the Lord God to grow every tree that is pleasant to the sight, and good for food; the tree of life also in the midst of the garden, and the tree of knowledge of good and evil. 10. And a river went out of Eden to water the garden; and from thence it was parted, and became into four heads. 11. The name of the first is Pison: that is it which compasseth the whole land of Havilah, where there is gold; 12. And the gold of that land is good: there is bdellium and the onyx stone. 13. And the name of the second river is Gihon: the same is it that compasseth the whole land of Ethiopia. 14. And the name of the third river is Hiddekel: that is it which goeth toward the east of Assyria. And the fourth river is Euphrates. 15. And the Lord God took the man, and put him into the garden of Eden to dress it and to keep it. 16. And the Lord God commanded the man, saying, Of every tree of the garden thou mayest freely eat: 17. But of the tree of the knowledge of good and evil, thou shalt not eat of it: for in the day that thou eatest thereof thou shalt surely die."*

Verse 8—Man was put in the Garden of Eden after his creation. Being that Adam was created outside the garden and afterwards placed inside the garden, there must have been an inside-the-garden and an outside-the-garden boundary. However inferred, Adam was to keep to the bounds of the garden and maintain the order of God's creation, Spirit-led and obedient to those limits.

The New Testament portrays the believer as being in the world but not of the world. There seems to be an admonishment here to maintain holiness and sanctification, as per New Testament teaching. The Garden of Eden was that place where God communed with man, accordingly, as man conformed to God's order. Conformity equates to obedience.

There was a veil, or separation, between Spirit–God and physical man. God is Spirit, immortal, celestial, and incorruptible. Man was none of these things. Man was flesh. Again, Eden was that place where man, while in order, was privileged to countenance with his creator. Thin was the veil in the time of mankind's innocence.

Verse 9 states, *"The tree of life also in the midst of the garden, and the tree of knowledge of good and evil."* These two trees are mentioned in conjunction with the other trees. No distinction is noted. Later, in Genesis 3:6, *"The woman saw that the tree was good for food, and that it was pleasant to the eyes, and a tree to be desired to make one wise."*

Two tree-features that Eve desired related to all the trees in the garden: *"Pleasant to the sight, and good for food."* That later statement, *"to make one wise"* (Genesis 3:6), was not a feature of the other trees.

Verse 15—*"And the Lord God took the man, and put him into the garden of Eden to dress it and to keep it."*

Repeating a previous mention: Verse 8 placed man in the garden. Here it gives the responsibilities of dressing and keeping it. To keep the garden would include keeping it clear of any threat or violation of God's commandments.

Verse 16—*"And the Lord God commanded the man, saying, Of every tree of the garden* <u>thou mayest freely eat:</u>*"* Man is given a do, or free-to-do commandment. We see no problem resulting from that freedom.

In verse 17, man is required to deal with his first *"thou shalt not."* And with the commandment went the statement of penalty. To wit: *"But of the tree of the knowledge of good and evil,* <u>thou shalt not</u> *eat of it: for in the day that thou eatest thereof* <u>thou shalt surely die.</u>*"*

Genesis 2:18–25—18. *"And the Lord God said, It is not good that the man should be alone; I will make him an help meet for him. 19. And out of the ground the Lord God formed every beast of the field, and every fowl of the air; and brought them unto Adam to see what he would call them: and whatsoever Adam called every living creature, that was the name thereof. 20. And Adam gave names to all cattle, and to the fowl of the air, and to every beast of the field; but for Adam there was not found an help meet for him. 21. And the Lord God caused a deep sleep to fall upon Adam, and he slept: and he took one of his ribs, and closed up the flesh instead thereof; 22. And the rib, which the Lord God had taken from man, made he a woman, and brought her unto the man. 23. And Adam said, This is now bone of my bones, and flesh of my flesh: she shall be called Woman, because she was taken out of Man. 24. Therefore shall a man leave his father and his mother, and shall cleave unto his wife: and they shall be one flesh. 25. And they were both naked, the man and his wife, and were not ashamed."*

Verse 18 declares God's awareness and intent that Adam needed a wife and would have a wife. *"And the Lord God said, It is not good that the man should be alone; I will make him an help meet for him."* Verses 19 and 20 demonstrate that none of the created animals, beast or fowl, would suffice. 19. *"And out of the ground the Lord God formed every beast of the field, and every fowl of the air; and brought them unto Adam to see what he would call them: and whatsoever Adam called every living creature, that was the name thereof. 20. And Adam gave names to all cattle, and to the fowl of the air, and to every beast of the field; but for Adam there was not found a help meet for him."*

Next, in verses 21 thru 25, we read the beautiful narrative of Woman's creation, and of her place with Adam, and their innocence. *"And the Lord God caused a deep sleep to fall upon Adam, and he slept: and he took one of his ribs, and closed up the flesh instead thereof; And the rib, which the Lord God had taken from man, made he a woman, and brought her unto the man. And Adam said, This is now bone of my bones, and flesh of my flesh: she shall be called Woman, because she was taken out of Man. Therefore shall a man leave his father and his mother, and shall cleave unto his wife: and they shall be one flesh. And they were both naked, the man and his wife, and were not ashamed."*

Verse 24 speaks regarding a man leaving father and mother; which course was God's ongoing intent for mankind. That particular matter of requirement was established from the beginning. This statement is quoted by Jesus and Paul in Matthew 19:5 and Ephesians 5:31, respectively.

God rested on the seventh day. God was pleased with his creation, having put into Adam's trust all things pertaining to the Garden of Eden. Did all proceed well from that point forward? No, it did not. How long did things go well? Not a foolish question, especially in light of chronological studies. Scripture is not explicit on that point.

Adam and Eve, as innocents, dwelt in the garden for an unstated time. Some say thirty years. Possibly; but, if that idea is speculative, then how long? We are aware that Jesus was thirty years of age when he was *"tempted of the devil"* (Matthew 4:1). Jesus was the *"last Adam"* (1 Corinthians 15:45). However detailed regarding the time factor, the Christ–Adam comparable is a bonified similitude.

Interpreting the Report: Literal or Allegorical?

Genesis chapters 1 thru 3 is a true report of an actual event. The parable of the rich man and Lazarus was truth, but <u>not</u> an actuality. Again, the report of Adam and Eve was true and it <u>was</u> an actuality.

Going forward, a foundational question arises. Is the story to be taken literally or, in whole or part, reported in an allegorical style, or even as a sort of parable? Reasonably, the narrative could be partly literal and partly figurative or allegorical.

While this narrative does not say that man was a tree or a tree was a man, a similitude is possible. Psalms 1:3 speaks of the blessed <u>man</u> and uses the simile: *"And he shall be <u>like a tree</u> planted by the rivers of water."* Proverbs 3:18 speaks of <u>wisdom</u> and uses the metaphor: *"She <u>is a tree</u> of life to them that lay hold upon her: and happy is every one that retained her."* Other like examples are given in Scripture, especially metaphors referring to fruit. *"The <u>fruit of the righteous</u> <u>is a tree of life</u>"* (Proverbs 11:30). Also, <u>desire</u>: *"When the desire cometh, it <u>is a tree of life</u>"* (Proverbs 13:12).

Was the Garden of Eden literal? Yes. Rereading Genesis 2:10–14, moves us in that direction. Next question: Is it lawful to express ideas of purpose and sanctity regarding that geographical place? Yes.

Now to the next question: Are we to treat the trees, the fruits of the trees, and the serpent as literal or allegorical? That question gives pause. We do not want to add to, or take away from the stated Word of God. Neither do we want to take away from the intended message, or marginalize, or deny the exemplary instruction we might receive from man's earliest record.

Messages given in allegorical form prompt greater in-depth thought processing. Allegories, or similitudes, paint pictures in our minds that are "worth more than a thousand words." That awareness, in itself, offers no proof as to the principals in the Garden of Eden record being similitude-like or literal. However, it does reflect the possible loss of insights otherwise gained by unveiling the allegories relating to the aforementioned five principals. If the text is treated literally, then there is a straightforward gleaning of the cause–effect principles of the event as set forth.

Moses has the right of authorship of the Book of Genesis. He received the report of the beginnings and downfall of man. We all believe God protects his Word so that it is neither corrupted nor embellished. Receiving or reporting the narrative as literal, or as part allegorical, was Moses' lot and his prerogative, respectively, as per God's direction.

If the sin in the garden was lust-driven and sensual, then the portrayal of their conduct might be judged unrepeatable by reporter Moses. Explicit reporting might offend the conscience of reporter and reader alike. God may have ordained that a similitude relate the event, veiled but complete. Knowing the God-ordained magnitude and circulation of the reported event, God could have rendered the accounting as allegorical and better suited for this widely published historical Bible narrative. As King Solomon wrote; *"It is the glory of God to conceal a thing; but the honour of kings is to search out a matter"* (Proverbs 25:2).

A personal note: It may seem improbable that we can accept the narrative as literal, and yet proceed to generate a truth-rendering of the matter as a present truth interpretation. That would mean that we leave the trees, fruits of the trees, and the serpent literal, as stated. However improbable, it is effectual, because of our obedience to the Lord's way of teaching, and because we embrace his expressions. It would be a serious error to entertain, in our spirit and in our thoughts, that we could have better stated the narrative. Accurately interpreting Scripture is good and needful. Exalting over scriptural presentation is not good.

If the report is accepted as an actuality and literally related, then New Testament revelation would yield the enlightened, meant-to-be interpretation; all God-ordered for our edification. That reasoning is the intention, and a "settlement," of a sort, regarding this article.

It is a certainty that ideas of purpose and sanctity, relating to the Genesis narrative, must be acceptable in light of the New Testament revelation. That is, a man may be likened to a tree in-order, or as a tree out-of-order. In-order is *"fruit unto holiness, and the end everlasting life"* (Romans 6:22). Out-of-order is no fruit, or fruit unto *"ashamed"* and *"death"* (Romans 6:21). Jesus is the perfect in-order example of whom we subscribe wholly. That is, we eat his flesh and drink his blood. He is a tree of life. His true disciples are likewise, trees of life. Again, rest assured, New Testament understanding will provide as great a revelation of truth if we treat the event of sin as reported; literal trees, literal fruits, and literal serpent. Freedom to glean from the reporting of a literal event, as given, is no loss.

The reported failure of the first man and woman is emblematic of all human frailty. Lacking the provision of God's redemptive grace, the penalty of sin is an ongoing estate of dying and the eventual event of death.

Genesis 3

Genesis 3:1—*"Now the serpent was more subtle than any beast of the field which the Lord God had made. And he said unto the woman, Yea, hath God said, Ye shall not eat of every tree of the garden?"*

This chapter starts off on an unlikely note, as per the carnal or unbelieving. A parrot may talk, but not a snake. To that we say, a donkey talked to Balaam, and it was, for certain, a literal event. The event here reveals two things. The serpent was subtle and the woman listened. Both are prime ingredients for deception. We believe the event happened. Literal or allegorical; we believe wholly that this narrative is related truthfully and without corruption.

Taken literally, we deduce: Snakes are dumb and so was Balaam's donkey. There had to be an intellect speaking thru those dumb creatures. Taken allegorically, the serpent could have been her fleshly desire driving her. How well do we know that desire can talk, as per its prompting? Our thoughts and cogitations are regularly verbalized.

Genesis 3:2–13—2. *"And the woman said unto the serpent, We may eat of the fruit of the trees of the garden: 3. But of the fruit of the tree which is in the midst of the garden, God hath said, Ye shall not eat of it, neither shall ye touch it, lest ye die. 4. And the serpent said unto the woman, Ye shall not surely die: 5. For God doth know that in the day ye eat thereof, then your eyes shall be opened, and ye shall be as gods, knowing good and evil. 6. And when the woman saw that the tree was good for food, and that it was pleasant to the eyes, and a tree to be desired to make one wise, she took of the fruit thereof, and did eat, and gave also unto her husband with her; and he did eat. 7. And the eyes of them both were opened, and they knew that they were naked; and they sewed fig leaves together, and made themselves aprons. 8. And they heard the voice of the Lord God walking in the garden in the cool of the day: and Adam and his wife hid themselves from the presence of the Lord God amongst the trees of the garden. 9. And the Lord God called unto Adam, and said unto him, Where art thou? 10. And he said, I heard thy voice in the garden, and I was afraid, because I was naked; and I hid myself. 11. And he said, Who told thee that thou wast naked? Hast thou eaten of the tree, whereof I commanded thee that thou shouldest not eat? 12. And the man said, The woman whom thou gavest to be with me, she gave me of the tree, and I did eat. 13. And the Lord God said unto the woman, What is this that thou hast done? And the woman said, The serpent beguiled me, and I did eat."*

We have no record as to who originally instructed Eve with respect to the fruit of the tree in the midst of the garden; probably Adam. Whether she added, *"Neither shall ye touch it, lest ye die"* (verse 3), we do not know. Again, possibly Adam added that part and it may have been stated in God's original warning and not recorded. Adam may have added it as a gesture; protective toward his wife. Indications are that God communed with <u>both</u> Adam and his wife. Verse 8 states, *"And <u>they</u> heard the voice of the Lord God walking in the garden."* Possibly God added that part, if and when he instructed her. Suffice to say, after having been instructed, she was deceived into believing the penalty would be mitigated, or worse, that the commandment was a lie. The serpent lied. *"Ye shall not surely die"* (verse 4). That perception persists today, and it is akin to the belief that the souls of all men are immortal.

Repeating verse 6. *"And when the woman saw that the tree was good for food, and that it was pleasant to the eyes, and a tree to be desired to make one wise, she took of the fruit thereof, and did eat, and gave also unto her husband with her; and he did eat."* And now . . . sin and death lie on the horizon.

From the text, it is clear that she eventually conformed to her creature wants. The serpent is portrayed as the influence causal in moving her to sin. The desire factor was in play from the onset. That sensual part; *"The tree was* good for food, *and that it was* pleasant to the eyes, *and a tree to be* desired to make one wise*"* (verse 6). If pride is "the mother of all sin," as some say, we can be sure the third mentioned, "pride of life" was primary. They desired to *"be as gods, knowing good and evil"* (verse 5).

As shown above, three root sins were in play: *"For all that is in the world, the* lust of the flesh, *and the* lust of the eyes, *and the* pride of life, *is not of the Father, but is of the world"* (1 John 2:16).

Eve was in the transgression. *"Adam was not deceived, but the woman being deceived was in the transgression"* (1 Timothy 2:14). Initially, she was without Adam, at least not being mentioned, in her transgression; howbeit, Adam was there.

Literal or otherwise, the fruit taken was her desire fulfilled, yielding death. Her action violated God's commandment. She then gave to her husband. She first, and then together they sinned, losing the fruit of righteousness, which was their covering; their original in-order estate. When they were in order, with their spirit being foremost, the Spirit of God covered them. God's Spirit relates to spirit in man, not to flesh. *"So then they that are in the flesh cannot please God"* (Romans 8:8).

They were naked, and they knew it. No longer fashioned after the tree of life, they were fashioned after the tree of the knowledge of good and evil. Flesh-driven and sensual, the soul of man subordinated in disobedience, and the spirit of man was covered over with flesh and brought to a state of unbelief. Result: A perverted order of first, flesh or body; second, soul; and, then last, spirit. That is, the spirit of man, once alive-to-God is covered by flesh. A New Testament similitude applicable to this first couple would be, *"Thy circumcision is made uncircumcision"* (Romans 2:25). They had given themselves to the creature desire, which was their fruit unto death. Again, the fruit of the tree of the knowledge of good and evil: Death. Henceforth, they were servants to the creature. Their blessed estate of being in service to the Creator was lost.

The cause of man's fall was his sensual, willful, and unbelieving actions contrary to God's intent, grace, and benevolence. Call their now present estate "first heaven," the estate of fallen mankind. Not a corporation, or entity created by the state, but a creation of man's doing and his demise. It would be legally termed an *unnatural body*. As per New Testament understanding, the finally realized "body of death." The pain of death prevails in man's "first heaven."

Verse 7—*"And the eyes of them both were opened, and they knew that they were naked; and they sewed fig leaves together, and made themselves aprons."*

Fig leaves provided no better covering than the unworthiness of Cain's offering *"of the fruit of the ground"* (Genesis 4:3). They were uncovered and they knew it. God knew it. And God knew that they knew it. There was no contest, and nothing hidden. The man and the woman tried to hide themselves. They were "helpless." Pride-driven and, as in death,"helpless."

Adam, in the state of innocence, was in the fashion of the tree of life. His estate was good and the order of his being, life, was right. He knew of the presence, in the Garden of Eden, of the evil tree and his option of refusing, or agreeing to know, experientially, the knowledge of that evil. Adam knew the penalty. He was not deceived. Eve was deceived and the party of immediate fault, but Adam yielded knowingly to the proposition, as per her persuasion.

Repeating Genesis 3:9–13—9. *"And the Lord God called unto Adam, and said unto him, Where art thou? 10. And he said, I heard thy voice in the garden, and I was afraid, because I was naked; and I hid myself. 11. And he said, Who told thee that thou wast naked? Hast thou eaten of the tree, whereof I commanded thee that thou shouldest not eat? 12. And the man said, The woman whom thou gavest to be with me, she gave me of the tree, and I did eat. 13. And the Lord God said unto the woman, What is this that thou hast done? And the woman said, The serpent beguiled me, and I did eat."*

It is noteworthy that God still communicated with them in their fallen state. Verse 8 states, *"They heard the voice of the Lord God walking in the garden in the cool of the day"* (or, as in several passages, in the wind or spirit). Their spirits may not have been severed from God's Spirit at that time. However, the separation was certainly evidenced at the time of their expulsion from the garden. The Garden of Eden was the place of Creator–creature communion; the place of God's Spirit connection with man's spirit. (Presently, the Church serves to reflect that blessed estate; a spiritual similitude. See Chapter IV, Second Heaven Estate.)

We know the New Testament speaks of demons and evil spirits of affliction, influence, and control. We can see the possibility that there was also present an individuality of influence or persuasion. The serpent was indeed present, be it fleshly desire speaking as from within, or an outside-the-body actuality.

Sin was perceived, revealed, then attached to Adam and Eve, and they were ashamed. Adam had yielded to Eve. Eve blamed the serpent, admitting that she was beguiled.

Judgments Pronounced

Genesis 3:14, 15—14. *"And the Lord God said unto the serpent, Because thou hast done this, thou art cursed above all cattle, and above every beast of the field; upon thy belly shalt thou go, and dust shalt thou eat all the days of thy life: 15. And I will put enmity between thee and the woman and between thy seed and her seed; it shall bruise thy head and thou shalt bruise his heel."*

Verse 14 gives first mention of the phrase, *"thou art cursed."* Looking at the literal aspect:

We know the serpent, or snake, is a belly-crawling creature relegated to the dust. Although snakes may be tree dwellers or swimmers, their reproduction and primary dwelling is in the dust. Also, that species certainly lost the ability to converse with humans, if they ever had it. One difficulty with a literal exchange is the unlikelihood that God would, in any way, converse with a serpent. The overriding fact is that there was no conversation, but rather God's pronouncement or declaration.

Allowing that the story being reported was allegorical:

We do see fleshly desire and fulfillment of things sensual, being relegated to the hidden or unseen; the shame factor. Only among those reprobate and lacking God-conscience, do we see the unashamed, uninhibited lifestyle. Relative to the cattle and beast of the field, only man suffers this affliction. This kind of sensuality likely pertains to more than eating, good for food, or looking, pleasant to the eyes.

Verse 15 declares enmity between the seed of the serpent and the seed of the woman. It is difficult to literalize this passage. Admittedly, the seed of the woman is literally the righteous line. The seed of the serpent would have to be the product, called seed of Eve, following her fleshly desires, as per the serpent's prompting. Reworded: Eve's desire-driven actions resulted in a generation of people that were contrary to God.

Both the Old and New Testaments follow the righteous line. In the New Testament, we see the fulfillment of the *"enmity"* pronouncement. *"Thy seed"* was the unrighteous, or evil. *"Her seed"* was the righteous line, fulfilled in Jesus. This was established, and the event of bruising the serpent's head culminated on the cross. Jesus died and rose from the dead, justified and glorified. His heel was bruised. Evil was relegated to the rank of totally unjustified. The head of the serpent was bruised. Evil was cast further from the presence of or from reconciliation with God. That was, as per Jesus' statement, *"For the prince of this world cometh, and hath nothing in me"* (John 14:30). *"Thy seed,"* the unrighteous line, and *"the prince of this world"* were totally unjustified in killing our Lord.

Genesis 3:16—*"Unto the woman he said, I will greatly multiply thy sorrow and thy conception; in sorrow thou shalt bring forth children; and thy desire shall be to thy husband, and he shall rule over thee."*

God declares to the woman the severe difficulty she is to bear. There is a world of medical expertise given to this area of sorrow. These are literal pronouncements and they are truly a suffering point for women. On this point, howbeit subtle, a complaint against God might be at the heart of the freedom-of-choice movement, be it knowingly or ignorant. Abortion is certainly contrary to the commandment to be fruitful and multiply and replenish the earth.

God states that Eve's *"desire shall be to thy husband."* We correctly see her desiring his physical comfort, protection, and/or fulfillment. Regarding these desires, the man is the aggressor and the woman is passive. Basic physiology speaks to that inclination. The man needs rule in these areas.

We also understand that she desired to rule over him. The immediate added comment was *"and he shall rule over thee."*

Adam had harkened to his wife and this breech of family order allowed the action of rebellion against God's commandment. Pride and self-determination were two factors causal in her desire to rule or lead him. Pertaining to humanity, this event reveals the origin and the pith and marrow of witchcraft. *"For rebellion is as the sin of witchcraft, and stubbornness is as iniquity and idolatry"* (1 Samuel 15:23). It was manifest disobedience. And, it was manifestly out of order.

Practitioners of evil do not always know the magnitude of an out-of-order relationship or the severe consequences of a singular act of this kind of sin. Thankfully, persons that do this kind of evil do not usually fit the classification of witch or warlock. Good people occasionally do evil things. In Church, family, job, or government, continuing in this kind of out-of-order stubbornness is sin. Adam and Eve lived the rest of their life in out-of-order sin. Eve's course of action resulted in the onset of "enmity." Her "sarx" behavior violated God's "creative intent."

Genesis 3:17–19—17. *"And unto Adam he said, Because thou hast hearkened unto the voice of thy wife, and hast eaten of the tree, of which I commanded thee, saying, Thou shalt not eat of it: cursed is the ground for thy sake; in sorrow shalt thou eat of it all the days of thy life; 18. Thorns also and thistles shall it bring forth to thee; and thou shalt eat the herb of the field; 19. In the sweat of thy face shalt thou eat bread, till thou return unto the ground; for out of it wast thou taken: for dust thou art, and unto dust shalt thou return."*

Adam was not deceived as by a serpent or other. His sin was harkening to his wife and subsequently eating of the tree of the knowledge of good and evil. Adam was not cursed. The curse he suffered was that the ground would yield thorns and thistles. Adam's diet would be herbs and that yield would be laborious. As a mark of the curse, God reminds Adam that the ground would be his end.

Genesis 3:20, 21—20. *"And Adam called his wife's name Eve; because she was the mother of all living. 21. Unto Adam also and to his wife did the Lord God make coats of skins, and clothed them."*

Adam and Eve faced a life of sorrow. Having been rebuked of God, they suffered the loss of all that would have perpetuated their eternal life and happiness. They went from the garden as lost souls.

God, in his mercy, made them coats of skins. I said mercy because the skins were produced from a slain animal. Hopefully, for their sakes, it was a clean animal, according to yet to be stated standards. Be it a clean animal or otherwise, we have no other indications or statements of any provision for their reconciliation.

Generally speaking, a clean animal sacrifice is a reflection of the love of God to be extended to mankind thru the sacrifice of his Son, Jesus Christ. Until the advent of Christ and the cross, any sacrifice was in type. Before and according to the Law, the giving of a proper sacrifice, with accountability, might allow that the participant heir a resurrection.

This clothing gesture is the only idea of hope for Adam and Eve. The opinion of most is that God's mercy did not extend to them. The concluding verses in this chapter indicate that they were eternally lost.

Genesis 3:22–24—22. *"And the Lord God said, Behold, the man is become as one of us, to know good and evil: and now, lest he put forth his hand, and take also of the tree of life, and eat, and live for ever: 23. Therefore the Lord God sent him forth from the garden of Eden, to till the ground from whence he was taken. 24. So he drove out the man; and he placed at the east of the garden of Eden cherubims, and a flaming sword which turned every way, to keep the way of the tree of life."*

The lot of all mankind, until Jesus, was, as the psalmist David said, *"I was shapen in iniquity; and in sin did my mother conceive me"* (Psalms 51:5). We have known good and evil. That is the case, whether there was a Bathsheba event or not. The fact is, we were all without hope. Even the righteous line, in itself, offered no remedy outside the prophesied Christ and his atoning blood.

The Bible record of man's creation and fall, and the result, should move us to thank God for redemption's plan. Simply put, thank God for Jesus. A thankfulness from the heart, knowing biblically of the onset of damnation.

Adam and Eve were driven from the garden, and his lot was to till the ground for his livelihood.

The entry to the garden was on the east side as was the Tabernacle in the wilderness. There is where God placed the *"cherubims, and a flaming sword which turned every way, to keep the way of the tree of life."*

The Tabernacle in the wilderness depicts the plan of salvation. Again, it faced east. It was not part of the desert, but it was in a desert place. It was a sanctified place, as was the Garden of Eden. In our dispensation of Grace, we are a sanctified tabernacle; in the world, but not of the world. In the beginning, the Garden of Eden was such a place. It was man's sanctified, hallowed habitation, fitting for man's communion with his Creator.

The flaming sword kept Adam and Eve from reentry and salvation. Hebrews 4:12 states, *"For the word of God is quick, and powerful, and sharper than any two-edged sword, piercing even to the dividing asunder of the soul and spirit."* With Adam and Eve, it was a sword of separation. Their fallen order was flesh–soul–spirit. Again, God does not have ongoing communion with a flesh-driven soul.

Before sin, *"The Spirit itself beareth witness with our spirit, that we are the children of God"* (Romans 8:16). They had oneness with God. After sin, the commandment, word, sword of God, went forth. They became victims of transgression. The order was perverted as a result of creature lust. Themselves, their souls, were estranged from God. Flesh became a barrier between God's Spirit and man's spirit.

With us, under the shed blood of Jesus, the word of God is a sword of separation of the flesh from our hearts. It is typified as circumcision. It is God's provision of life for us thru the shed blood of Jesus Christ. That is a place in God worth all cost. Paul gives perfect perspective: *"For the flesh lusteth against the Spirit, and the Spirit against the flesh: and these are contrary the one to the other: so that ye cannot do the things that ye would"* (Galatians 5:17). The benefit of obedience: God's life; *"He that is joined unto the Lord is one spirit"* (1 Corinthians 6:16). That was good order and good communion: Spirit–spirit of man, soul, body.

Individual salvation and redemption constitute a reversal, or spin, from body–soul–spirit to a spirit–soul–body order. That is not ours alone to determine or accomplish. It is an operation of the Holy Ghost. Jesus said, *"No man can come to me, except the Father which hath sent me draw him"* (John 6:44).

Concerning Curses and Punishment: Revisit Genesis 3:14–19
Enmity: The "Mother Curse" of Fallen Humanity

The serpent conflicted with God's plan. Verses 14 and 15 reveal "enmity" to be the product of Eve's deception, and the serpent is portrayed as causal. *Enmity* is fundamentally the harsh separation of Creator and creature. That being the case, enmity continues as the root of the continuing rift between the righteous line and the ungodly. As understood by New Testament revelation; enmity between the world and the Saints.

James 4:1–4— 1. *"From whence come wars and fightings among you? Come they not hence, even of your lusts that war in your members? 2. Ye lust and have not: ye kill, and desire to have, and cannot obtain: ye fight and war, yet ye have not, because ye ask not. 3. Ye ask, and receive not, because ye ask amiss, that ye may consume it upon your lusts. 4. Ye adulterers and adulteresses, know ye not that the friendship of the world is enmity with God? Whosoever therefore will be a friend of the world is the enemy of God."*

More precisely, the apostle James is referring to wars in the Church. However, in the overview, the same holds true in the world and among nations. The serpent was the instigator of enmity; primarily, enmity between God and man. We can also understand that the serpent is responsible for enmity among nations and persons. Enmity is a prime ingredient for war. Enmity also prevails between the righteous line, the church, and the unrighteous line, the world.

New Testament records show that enmity in the Church is causal for rebellion, overturning of God's order, and loss of souls. Enmity is serious and consequential. It may result in variances between God-ordained leadership and a not-so-spiritual laity, and vice versa.

Please take note. Old Testament records show the dreadful price of enmity and lust. These iniquities corrupted the unity between God's appointed mediator, Moses, and the people. The term *iniquity* is used because the sin went against, and perverted, the order of God. Sin and the resulting rebellion caused the diminishing of God's preferred order: The order of the firstborn. The children of Israel made a golden calf and engaged in lustful idolatrous worship. Moses broke the first finger-of-God writings on tables of stone (Exodus 32:16, 19). While Aaron had failed, *"all the sons of Levi gathered themselves unto him"* (verse 26). That is, they gathered themselves unto Moses. A Levite also responded, in like manner, in the incident involving Phinehas' zeal for the Lord (Numbers 25:12). Historically, Levi, with Simeon, were enforcers (Genesis 34:25). The order of the firstborn was replaced, as in service to Aaron, by the Levitical order. It was Moses, not God this second time, who *"hewed two tables of stone like unto the first"* (Exodus 34:4). If we can comprehend the overview: The firstborn was essentially sacrificial in redeeming Israel. The whole of the tribe of Levi ascended to the post of enforcer. It was centralization in one tribe. No longer were there lights in every family. The firstborn became the past order and lights went out all across that nation. That was good as God's required justice, but not his intended best. This is a root problem, even the curse of organization. It was a penalty allowed, even prescribed, by the Lord. The product of enmity: Centralization. It was leadership in the hands of an oligarchy. While the whole tribe of Levi was chosen, a relatively few controlled the tribe. The sadness we see is that the glory was taken from families and caused to rest in a few. (Hebrews 12:23 reflects a healing of the breech: *"church of the firstborn."*)

A similitude of a transferred offering, or substitution, is shown by the offering of the ram instead of Isaac (Genesis 22:13). The Law was added, or first instituted, then Grace. That sequence is stated plainly in Galatians 3:19: *"It (Law) was added because of transgression."*

Enmity is a spiritual feature. Where enmity prevails, there is no communion. Primarily, there is a loss of communion between God and man. After that, there is loss of communion among nations and persons. Furthermore, there is loss of faith and loss of the Spirit connection. From that proceeds death and hell. The curse of the "pale horse: *and his name that sat on him was Death, and Hell followed with him*" (Revelation 6:8).

Verse 16 speaks to Eve. She is under the curse of enmity. Sadly, hostility and separation are her sorrows. Her pain and suffering, both physical and emotional, are abiding sorrows. She was moved, at the serpent's prompting, to satisfy her desire. Now, her desire was to her husband. She further sorrowed, observing her husband's unending toil to provide the basics for their existence. A confusion factor as a continuing enmity likely accompanied her God-instilled love for her husband.

While Eve is a singular person, the curse of enmity starts with her deception. Enmity is causal for war, destruction, and death.

Note: If the Bible student will pursue the study; the insight gained is to understand that *iniquity* is sin that is "flavored with 'enmity,'" in the most dreadful and consequential sense.

Dominion Lost

Adam lost control of his habitat. Simply stated and understood, the plant kingdom and the animal kingdom were no longer subordinate to him. He ceased to be "Spirit-motivated" and became "creature-driven." Adam and Eve and all mankind, from the time sin entered, were in servitude to all that surrounded them. In the broad spectrum, they became servants to sin. In terms of world order, "self-serving" constituted a principal ingredient for war.

The product of this curse, loss of dominion, pertaining to the plant kingdom, is famine. Famine relates to the black horse. "*Lo a **black horse**; and he that sat on him had a pair of balances in his hand. And I heard a voice in the midst of the four beast say, A measure of wheat for a penny, and three measures of barley for a penny*" (Revelation 6:6). As pertained to the animal kingdom, micro and macro, disease and pestilence. Pestilence and disease follow with famine, hostility, and sorrow.

Enmity with Dominion Lost

Enmity, or hostility and stress among nations, when added to world poverty, are enhancements for an atmosphere of war and the sword. The loss of God-ordained leading, intuition, and dominion leaves nations naked. With communion lost and misconnections numerous, progressing forward, God removed his hand of covering and forthwith, the nations or tribal peoples go to war. Killing with any instrument of war will suffice. If the sword is the weapon of choice, so be it, and we read it in the Bible, "*Another **horse that was red**: and power was given to him that sat thereon to take peace from the earth, and that they should kill one another: and there was given unto him a great sword*" (Revelation 6:4).

Redemption: Revelation's Overturning, Overturning, Overturning

The Lord God created this world and he instituted the behavior required of mankind. Mankind failed, and forthwith God instituted the course of penalty and correction. The course and manner of righting the wrong is embodied in the penalties. To wit: War, famine, pestilence, and, death and hell. *"And I saw, and behold a* **white horse**: *and he that sat on him had a bow; and a crown was given unto him: and he went forth conquering, and to conquer"* (Revelation 6:2).

Jesus rides the white horse, going forth, in this end time, conquering and to conquer. He orchestrates the restitution. Jesus has ordained by his life and sacrifice, the penalties and corrections. Ordained of God, he has the promises of restoration in hand.

The sword, at the garden entrance, was for separation. "In Christ" and among the chosen, the sword of separation is unto sanctification. He now wields the sword; not for war, but to judge and separate the citizenry of the world-to-come from this present world. His sword is for our spiritual circumcision unto eternal life. Our blessing.

Jesus has a bow; the promises. We are under his wings. We need only to look up. There are eyes under those wings; the prophecies and promises of God. They are portals, as it were, into the third heaven's plan of God. *"Whereby are given unto us exceeding great and precious promises: that by these ye might be partakers of the divine nature, having escaped the corruption that is in the world through lust"* (2 Peter 1:4). They are precious promises of God's good intentions toward his chosen. Included is the promise, as did Jesus, to lead captivity captive. We are to lead captive the things that hitherto fore had led us captive. He wills that the believer rise above the world, pride, and fleshly lust.

Jesus Christ was sent to pay the price, a sacrifice for sin. Having accomplished that, he is set down on the right hand of God, his Father, in heaven. And, *"To him that overcometh will I grant to sit with me in my throne, even as I also overcame, and am set down with my Father in his throne"* (Revelation 3:22). *"To him that overcometh will I give to eat of the* tree of life, *which is in the midst of the paradise of God"* (Revelation 2:7).

Chart Representations

Order of Man As Created

Spirit–Soul–Body

Fallen Order of Man

Body–Soul–Spirit

God/Spirit relates to the spirit in man. A person Spirit-led; his spirit, by faith believing, serves the Creator. To wit:

God/Spirit does not relate to the body or flesh of a person. A person who is flesh-driven serves the creature. To wit:

Man, as a tree in-order, is a soul obedient to the Creator; a <u>tree of life</u>.	Man, as a tree out-of-order, is a soul disobedient to the Creator; a <u>tree of the knowledge of good and evil</u>.

Redemption's Plan

Sin in the Garden =	<u>Spirit</u>–Unbelief	<u>Soul</u>–Disobedience	<u>Body</u>–Flesh–Sensual
Penalty or Curse =	Enmity, Death	Lost Dominion	Pestilence, Famine

<u>Redemption is "In Christ." He rides the White Horse. He Conquers, Purges, and Restores via:</u>

<u>White Horse</u>	Pale Horse	Red Horse	Black Horse
<u>He has "the keys of hell and of death."</u>	Death/Hell	War/Sword	Pestilence/Famine

First, man had clear conscience toward God (Spirit). As such, Adam had eternal life. Also, he had dominion or leadership. Having such, man experienced no pestilence or famine. And, in as much as God is Spirit, man's uncorrupted spirit had Spirit–spirit communion; thus, no enmity. Adam was yielded to God's Law accordingly. As he was created: In God's image. Sensitivity, communion, and leading. God-given and, that by faith, no unbelief. These three features; conscience, dominion, and communion, are given in similitude, as articles in the Ark in the Holy of Holies. Respectively: The Law, the Rod that budded, and the golden pot of Manna.

Second, man had a mind, will, and emotion (soul) that was altogether subject, in obedience, to God's thinking, God's will, and God's feelings.

Third, Adam was given the mechanism (body) for his continuance or existence. This third part was the tabernacle or physical body. The body was not that part that qualified man as being *"in our image, after our likeness."* In Greek terminology, *Suma*, the body is not inherently evil. The body was certainly not created for evil. *Sarx* is flesh and may well be fitted to do and be evil. In terms of order, the body was the down under or subordinate part.

The <u>spirit</u> in man was to prevail uppermost in faithful connectivity with God. The person, <u>soul</u>, was to serve God's purpose being obedient. Again, the <u>body</u> was under and the <u>spirit</u> was uppermost. Thus, the <u>order</u> as per God's creation: <u>Spirit</u>, –<u>Soul</u>, –<u>Body</u>. Thus, the Creator, Spirit, is preeminent and the creature, soul, or person being Spirit-led, is servant to the Creator. The creation is subordinate to the Creator and creature, in that order. The reason being: The *creation*, material/physical, is the mechanism for continuance of mortal life. God's order: Creator/Spirit, –creature/soul, –creation/body.

In 1 Thessalonians 5:23, *"And the very God of peace sanctify you wholly; and I pray God your whole <u>spirit</u> and <u>soul</u> and <u>body</u> be preserved blameless unto the coming of our Lord Jesus Christ."*

Summary

Having slanted things toward the present truth, we are not prevented from accepting the narrative as given; literal trees, literal fruits, and a literal serpent. The original sin was a composite of sensual desire, disobedience, and faithlessness. That composite equates to the total man: Spirit, soul, and body. There is no offence in accepting the literal eating of fruit from a literal tree. Bottom line: The Genesis narrative is God's doing and Moses was giving the report exactly as God intended. If so be, the devil issue is locked out of the discussion. He, if he was there, should be locked out. Thus, being free of that contest, we see the narrative reported in good taste and complete.

In all, we thank God for the light of history and our New Testament understanding. All godly knowledge is the gift of God and imparted by the life and light of our Lord Jesus Christ and the Holy Ghost.

The serpent is reported to be a talking creature, an evil component. Being that the serpent was an evil component added to the narrative; possibly, fleshly desire was personified as a serpent. Thus, it could have come from Eve's body/fleshly desire, and influenced her thinking. Or, it could have been an outside-the-garden influence. The fact that Eve was deceived leaves inference that there could have been an outside influence. As already mentioned, Adam was not deceived. His initial fault was listening and responding to his wife. So being, they ate of the tree. It was in the midst of the garden. Literal or allegorical, it resulted in a physical, bodily action. Admittedly, the Song of Solomon alludes to the garden as relating to physical considerations. There are few such references, only poetic and only allegorical.

Did God create evil? Was evil somehow inherently a part of his creation? Evil is not reported, or alluded to, as being a part of creation. The next question: Would not an already existing evil necessarily have been introduced from without? The answer is a possible "no" to both questions. Consider. Adam and Eve were in God's image, and that would include creativity and freedom of choice. Those two features could account for the origin of an act that constituted evil. If so be, then, evil might not be a product of God's creativity or the introduction of an outside evil force. Be it a voice from within, or a voice from without, it included a prompting and the prompter was reported to be the serpent.

The answer and conclusion, as to the introduction of sin starting from within versus without, is not declared in the Genesis narrative.

The Old Testament history of the flood, and later the destruction of Sodom, gives clear and concise reporting of man's degradation and the sin in particular that was responsible. Thus, we necessarily go to Bible history and the subsequent disastrous conduct of humanity, and the resulting judgments. Therein rests the answer to what transpired, fundamentally, in bringing to pass this first heaven wherein we reside. That is a credible statement because the Genesis narrative is emblematic of sin's product. As for getting understanding and wisdom pertaining to the present, that desired end requires that we go to the light of the New Testament. And, it is critical that we gain knowledge and the wisdom pertaining to the present truth. This we do know, and repeat. Our present understanding regards the sin in the Garden of Eden as emblematic of the sin of yielding to the lust of the flesh, and disobedience, and unbelief. Thus, we see depicted, the fallen estate of mankind and this present world.

Man was created in the image of God. That allows for the oneness of man and his creator. Continuing communion was predicated and dependent on divine order. To wit: Since God is Spirit, man had to remain, as he was created, Spirit-led. That is, his spirit being foremost, above his bodily/fleshly wants and demands. Adam abode in that order. Simply put, his spirit communed with the Spirit of God. That was the connection: Spirit–spirit. To wit: Romans 8:16, *"The Spirit itself beareth witness with our spirit, that we are the children of God."* This may be termed a Spirit-motivated person. The person/soul was subject to the Creator and his body/flesh was subordinate. Scripture describes that battle line. *"For the flesh lusteth against the Spirit, and the Spirit against the flesh: and these are contrary the one to the other: so that ye cannot do the things that ye would"* (Galatians 5:17). Also, verse 24. *"And they that are Christ's have crucified the flesh with the affections and lust.* The *"ye"* and the *"they,"* is you, the person; the thinking, conscious man, or soul (psyche). Continuing communion requires that we be spirit-led.

Man was the highest order of God's creation. As created, man was obedience to his creator. As Spirit-motivated, his <u>faith</u> was intact and he was <u>obedient</u>, accounting the physical part, or body, as <u>under or subordinate</u>.

<u>Man, in this blessed estate/order, is like, or has become, a tree of life.</u> He is connected and in communion, with his creator. The <u>fruit is life and righteousness.</u>

Adam and Eve erred in their disobedience and, according to creature desires, gave priority to the flesh. At that point, the creature became a priority and the spirit connection was lost under fleshly lust and disobedience. *"Wherefore God also gave them up to uncleanness through the lusts of their own hearts, to dishonour their own bodies between themselves: who changed the truth of God into a lie, and worshipped and served the creature more than the Creator, who is blessed for ever Amen"* (Romans 1:24, 25).

<u>Mankind, in this disconnect/cursed order, became like a tree of the knowledge of good and evil. The fruit is shame and death.</u>

The serpent is reported to be a talking creature; an evil component. Whether the serpent was fleshly desire talking from within, or an outside-the-body influence, it exalted to influence and persuade man toward evil. Evil is demonstrated when spirituality is overtaken in terms of priority. That is, spirituality, or Spirit-led, suborns to pride-driven, carnal desire.

CHAPTER 3

Law

Treating God's Will and Intent, Violations and Resulting Impositions

THIS SECTION ADDRESSES THE basic premises of God's plan. It speaks to the progression of "law," as applied to man. It is helpful, even as a review, to understand that the plan of God is ongoing and progressive in the judgment scenario, and judgment is foundational. The treatment of "law" is integral to the doctrine of eternal judgment; starting with Adam, in his state of innocence, till the end, when all of mankind *"may be perfect and entire, wanting nothing"* (James 1:4). Predictably, some thoughts and expressions may be different from conventional teachings on the subject. Our purpose is to give insights corresponding with the study of God's intent, even being an encouragement to *"go on unto perfection"* (Hebrews 6:1). That is God's plan.

In the Perfect Economy, Law Is Inherent
As the Unity of Creator and Creature

"In the beginning God created the heaven and the earth" (Genesis 1:1). In the beginning was God alone, immortal and celestial. John 1:1 states, *"In the beginning was the Word, and the Word was with God, and the Word was God."* Word in the native idiom (Greek) is *logos*. As per: Philosophy and Theology/Britannica.com, it is defined as "reason" or "plan." In Greek philosophy and theology, "the divine reason implicit in the cosmos, ordering it and giving it form and meaning." Strong's Concordance states: *Logos*, something "said" including the "thought," a "topic," also "reasoning" or "motive." Regarding John 1:1: The Divine "expression" (i.e., Christ).

God's will, plan, reason, and law are inherently synonymous. And, as much as was humanly possible, it was synonymous in Adam. Correctly stated: The Law of God was innate in Adam. His spirit did approach a perfect state of being at-one with God's Spirit. Notwithstanding, Adam was a mortal, a terrestrial. However thin the veil between mortal and the immortal, there remained the veil. Only in the spirit can humankind traverse that veil. Jesus said of the Father *"God is a Spirit"* (John 4:24). On that point of difference-of-realms: Looking forward, the apostle Paul states, *"For now we see through a glass, darkly; but then face to face: now I know in part; but then shall I know even as also I am known"* (1 Corinthians 13:12).

Man's obedience was inherent, per his original created estate. There was no contest with God. There was no law, as a force or directive, applied toward Adam's will demanding obedience. Adam, in his innocence, was not subjected to law as a directive with demand for willful compliance to dos and don'ts. Adam's spiritual sensitivity-of-conscience was the directive. God's will was embraced as a matter of spirit-at-one-ment. Obedience was a matter of his conscience being sensitive and ordered by God.

This era could also be noted as "the dispensation of conscience," in that Adam lived according to that "dispensing," at creation, of a conscience void of offence. It was "the time of innocence."

Adam was at one with heaven's plan when he was placed in Eden. He was at one with his creator, without disobedience or other violations. As created, God's law was resident in his spirit, soul, and body, by virtue of his compliant spirit with and in God's Spirit. Originally, Adam was a partaker of the divine nature. Reasonably, Adam abode and rested in that estate. The same estate, touching innocence, we now occupy by imputed righteousness, *"in Christ."* In 2 Peter 1:4, it states, *"partakers of the divine nature."*

Mankind was in God's image. They were creative, with free will present, and tragically that twofold capacity gave rise to sin and death. He imagined, and then determined, or willed, to sin. God's commandment had gone forth: *"And the LORD GOD commanded the man, saying, Of every tree of the garden thou mayest freely eat: But of the tree of the knowledge of good and evil, thou shalt not eat of it: for in the day that thou eatest thereof thou shalt surely die"* (Genesis 2:16, 17).

With the advent of the breech of *"thou shalt not,"* Adam was separated from his Creator in the realm of spiritual affinity of man's spirit with God's Spirit. He fell from that estate. For Adam, in this instance, the word of God became a sword of separation, *"For the word of God is quick, and powerful, and sharper than any two-edged sword, piercing even to the dividing asunder of soul and spirit"* (Hebrews 4:12). *"The LORD GOD sent him forth from the garden of Eden"* (Genesis 3:23). Thereafter, Adam's spirit no longer bore witness with God's Spirit. God's law and intended obedience became a directive from without. We say "from without" because Adam was no longer in a unity of Spirit–spirit with God. Thus, we understand the basis of "Law" as it came to be perceived and experienced. To wit: Thereafter, obedience to law being accomplished primarily by the performance of will worship. Henceforth, man's era experienced the dispensing of "law and guilt; unmitigated." Man's conscience, being covered by the shroud of flesh, was dead to God. And, as saith the Scripture, depicting Adam's choice: *"Know ye not, that to whom ye yield yourselves servants to obey, his servants ye are to whom ye obey; whether of sin unto death or of obedience unto righteousness?"* (Romans 6:16).

The *"Word"* was in effect from the beginning, so that going forward, a righteous line was initiated by the faith of Able, who chose *"obedience unto righteousness."* Hebrews 11:4 states, *"By faith Abel offered unto God a more excellent sacrifice than Cain, by which he obtained witness that he was righteous,"* Abel offered a living sacrifice with blood; later his blood was shed. (Jesus initiated our purchase and sonship with his shed blood.) The verse continues, *"God testifying of his gifts: and by it he being dead yet speaketh."* God spoke his mind; reflecting the fundamental basis of resurrection, *"What hast thou done? the voice of thy brother's blood crieth unto me from the ground"* (Genesis 4:10). Pertaining to the righteous line, this was the time or era of "conscience, law and guilt; mitigated."

Being expelled from the Garden of Eden, Adam was no longer in the image of God. That equates to no longer having those God-like spiritual capacities of <u>communion with God</u>, <u>dominion given of God</u>, and <u>uncorrupted conscience toward God</u>.

Pertaining to the fallen estate of humankind, Adam can be thought of as the creator of this present world. Revelation 21:1 referred to it as *"the first heaven and the first earth"* where law prevails as God's finger of accusation. The same writer calls it *"the world"* (1 John 2:17). In that estate, the only means of doing obedience to God's Will is via the will of man, or as Paul states, *"the law of my mind"* (Romans 7:23).

The gift of life and perfection will not happen for us in-Adam and loving this present world. But, in-Christ, sanctified, it is happening with born-again believers. In-Christ; to wit: *"For if by one man's offence death reigned by one; much more they which receive abundance of grace and of the gift of righteousness shall reign in life by one, Jesus Christ"* (Romans 5:17).

Reiterating thoughts pertaining to spirit: Because of sin and the execution of God's word, commandment, and sword, Adam's <u>s</u>pirit was separated from God's <u>S</u>pirit. Adam essentially lost his God-given image of the creator: God likeness equates to three "spirit" features: communion, sensitivity of conscience, and dominion. Henceforth, Adam's creation, being first heaven, had fallen to an estate where obedience to God's will was a performance of the will of man. Sensitivity of conscience ceased to be the primary facilitator. That is, man's compromised sensitivity of conscience ceased to be the obedience factor.

From the time of the expulsion from the Garden of Eden until the advent of the Law of Moses, man willfully attempted to do obedience to God. With exceptions, this dispensation of conscience was essentially the dispensation of guilt, a guilty conscience. (Exceptions being those who, by faith, engaged in sacrifices, with blood, which was a similitude of the eventual offering of Jesus' life and blood. Jesus was prophetically, and now being, *"the Lamb slain from the foundation of the world"* (Revelation 13:8). They, especially the righteous line, embraced the promises, as being enlivened by faith. However, touching all of humanity, only with the advent of Jesus would it be said, *"Glory to God in the highest, and on earth peace, good will toward men"* (Luke 2:14).

Note: Some are of the opinion that, had Adam remained righteous and above law, he would have grown to maturity and perfection in the unity of spirit and knowledge of God. And, with maturity, perfection, possibly a path to immortality. Hypothetically, we might agree, but it did not happen with Adam.

The Law presently sits as the "judge" of "this world." That equates to this present world being in the estate of "unmitigated guilt." To wit: *"He that believeth on him is not condemned: but* <u>*he that believeth not is condemned already,*</u> *because he hath not believed in the name of the only begotten Son of God"* (John 3:18).

In due time, the "Law of Moses" was given as the more perfect finger of God, both accuser and blessing, toward man, particularly, the seed of Abraham and, especially, the righteous line. It was more perfect because it more perfectly defined and depicted sin. Romans 8 covers that premise.

The Law, As Pertaining to Moses

What saith the Law of Moses? Some may say, why ask? Is it not dead? Is it even to be considered? Aren't we now under the administration of Grace? Yes, but we are helped if we understand the cause, and the purpose, and the reason that the Law was given. We are benefited if we know the righteousness and fulfillment of the Law. Such an understanding shines light on our blessed estate of "Grace unto perfection." Again, yes; the Law is dead, but without an understanding of how it is dead, we risk being in violation of its righteousness; even discounting the Lord's fulfilling its righteousness. Consider it? A certain yes. Not only consider the Law, but with further discussion, understand that in-Christ, we have fulfilled the Law. Be assured that the Law will be resident and complete in anyone who attains to an overcoming life; perfection.

What is the Law? The finger of God wrote the Ten Commandments in the tablets of stone. Also, there were rituals, ordinances, offerings, and blood sacrifices. Beyond the commandments lay the hope of a more complete work of love: judgment, justification, and reconciliation. Relating to the Law of Moses, these commandments to "works" did proceed from heaven and did include the dispensing of limited spiritual communion, which communion was very select. In the overview, it was the dispensation of continued spiritual estrangement, wherein man was essentially, in spirit, separated from God. It was a continued dispensation of conscience (guilty conscience). The finality of that is death, with exceptions. Again, exceptions were those having faith with the hope of a resurrection, especially the righteous line. In terms of God's righteousness revealed through the mediation of Moses, it gave the believing Jew their "dispensation of the Law."

The "root" of the imposition of law goes to Adam: If he had lived above sin, God could have, even to the present, been revealed to us and in us. But, because man sinned, law was added. Later, for the sake of a nation, the Law pertaining to Moses was added. *"Wherefore then serveth the law? It was added because of transgressions, till the seed should come to whom the promise was made; and it was ordained by angels in the hand of a mediator"* (Galatians 3:19). Obviously, the context is the Law relating to Moses the *"mediator,"* and, at best, it only ameliorated sin's death sentence. Moses' Law was effective in resolving acts of committed sin in a fashion that would accommodate the vast company of Israel.

How Is the Law Fulfilled?

Do not err on this fact: While the Law was accusatory, it was righteous. It proceeded from a righteous God. This is the message of Romans 7:7–25, especially verse 12, *"Wherefore the law is holy, and the commandment holy, and just, and good."* Necessarily, and for the good of the nation of Israel, God's more effectual word of accusation, condemnation, and command was instituted. The faith of Abraham was both root and justification, so that God instituted this Law. It remained a sword of continued separation from God's inner sanctum. On the side of blessing, it was a sword of separation from the ungodly nations of that day and, foremost, a sword of sanctification; the similitude is "circumcision."

Going forward: Believers are now "in Christ." Jesus is our "rest," having been *"delivered from the law, that being dead wherein we were held; that we should serve in newness of spirit, and not in the oldness of the letter"* (Romans 7:6). The apostle Paul sounded a pastoral warning, *"Let us therefore fear, lest, a promise being left us of entering into his rest, any of you should seem to come short of it"* (Hebrews 4:1). Tragedy of tragedies if we should lose our Spirit-spirit communion with our Lord and with the Creator. *"The Spirit itself beareth witness with our spirit, that we are the children of God"* (Romans 8:16). Again, as saith the apostle Paul, *"He that is joined unto the Lord is one spirit"* (1 Corinthians 6:17). This blessed estate of sonship is to be embraced even unto perfection. To wit: *"In my Father's house are many mansions"* (John 14:2). "house" in this Scripture can rightfully equate to household or family. Commensurate with Jesus word is the apostle Paul's statement; *"But Christ as a son over his own house; whose house are we, if we hold fast the confidence and the rejoicing of the hope firm unto the end"* (Hebrews 3:6).

Restating the premise: The Law and the commandment proceeds from God; it is *"holy, and just, and good"* (Romans 7:12). To that, fearing God, we offer no contest. Fearing God, we continue, faithful in our embrace of Christ; that is, being a partaker of the righteousness of Christ. *"For he hath made him to be sin for us, who knew no sin; that we might be made the righteousness of God in him"* (2 Corinthians 5:21). Now, going forward as being "in Christ."

Romans 3:21, 22 states, *"But now the righteousness of God without law is manifested, being witnessed by the law and the prophets; Even the righteousness of God which is by faith of Jesus Christ unto all and upon all them that believe: for there is no difference."* (It is interesting to consider a literal manifestation of verse 21 witnessed on the Mount of Transfiguration. See Matthew 17:1–9. Moses representing the Law and Elijah representing the Prophets.) Repeating: Pertaining to Jesus and then us, the *"righteousness of God without law . . . unto all and upon all them that believe."* This is understood only in the sense that the law is fulfilled in Jesus and then imputed to us by faith. As Jesus said, *"Think not that I am come to destroy the law, or the prophets: I am not come to destroy, but to fulfill"* (Matthew 5:17). In this, Jesus, by his blood, opened the door for salvation and sanctification; the manifold Grace of God unto perfection. Enter: "The Dispensation of Grace." This is the blessed estate, where sin is not imputed to believers embracing the efficacy of Christ's shed blood. *"For the Father judgeth no man, but hath committed all judgment unto the son"* (John 5:22).

Hindsight concerning the Law: Now, as we best understand its original advent, "law" proceeded from violation. Sin. It proceeded from the necessity to declare, *"Thou shalt not."* After which, "The Law of Moses" was given. Thenceforth, the institution of ritualistic sacrifice. Offerings of this nature fulfilled the required "works of righteousness." Works that proceeded from a need for justification, as per the Law.

Considering the plight of the Adamic side: The root of the matter was that they were not sinners because they sinned; rather, they sinned because they were sinners. Reasonably, they were bound to "works" because of sin, and continuing in sin because they were sinners. Thus, that continuing cycle of bondage to the Law, sacrifice, and works. Jesus lived above these works. He was the "work" or complete Law. Resident in his body and life on the cross, was the Law. He rested because he was the Sabbath and the Law was dead, fulfilled in him. The Law's command to "works" was never applied to Christ's life. We will not enumerate the freedoms he exercised in that regard. Many. Expectedly, the Pharisees took exception.

Touching our salvation: We are complete in Him. When we, by faith, embrace Christ we become partakers of his righteousness. The works are resident in his sinless life and we are one with him. In him we rest from our works. By faith we fulfill the Law. By faith the works of the flesh are dead in us as they are in Christ. Now, we, by faith, reckon ourselves dead to sin. We, by faith, put our flesh on the cross and reckon the Law fulfilled in us. Thus, we are *"dead to the Law by the body of Christ"* (Romans 7:4). Thus, by faith in Christ is the Law dead that we may be freed from that bondage–works–sacrifice–law. *"Even as David also described the blessedness of the man, unto whom God imputed righteousness without works"* (Romans 4:6).

The Law continues, but fulfilled, in Jesus. *Fulfilled* is sometimes termed "dead." The Law continues, but fulfilled in us, as we are "in Christ." We are now freed from the Law of sin and death to move on to the righteousness of Grace. The Law that was unto death is now overtaken by righteousness. The covenant remains as a sort of schoolmaster, but we are under a new headship. It is Christ's righteousness. Let us not be as those *"being ignorant of God's righteousness, and going about to establish their own righteousness, have not submitted themselves unto the righteousness of God"* (Romans 10:3). *"For by grace are ye saved through faith; and that not of yourselves: it is the gift of God: Not of works, lest any man should boast"* (Ephesians 2:8, 9). The apostle Paul further states in 1 Corinthians 1:30, 31, *"But of him are ye in Christ Jesus, who of God is made unto us wisdom, and righteousness, and sanctification, and redemption: That, according as it is written, He that glorieth, let him glory in the Lord."*

In context: If you are "positionally" without sin, then of a certainty we are ordained to remain "in Christ" and go on to overcoming and perfection. Do not frustrate the Grace of God, *"Let us go on unto perfection"* (Hebrews 6:1). It is the Plan and Intent of God. That is God's manifest love wherein we abide.

Chart

It is the reader's opportunity and occasion to study this chart. As such, it is enlightening, considering the reader gives sufficient time and meditation to the twenty-eight compared items.

The two columns show transitions from Law to Grace. These things are not always obvious, but they reflect the graduation from Law to Grace. That "Graduation Plan" was facilitated by the dispensing of "Moses unto the Law" (column one) and then, the dispensing, from heaven, of "Christ unto Grace" (column two).

Moses	Christ
Law	Grace
Old Testament	New Testament
Moon	Sun
Light, Source Unseen	Light, Source Revealed

Servant	Son

Non-Abiding _____ Resident
Letter of the Law _____ Spirit
Levites _____ Firstborn
Aaron _____ Melchisedec
(Twenty-Four Elders) _____ (Four Living Creatures)
Morning/Evening Sacrifices _____ Pascal Sacrifice
Committed Sin _____ Original Sin
Earthly (Terrestrial Realm) _____ Heavenly (Celestial)
Observable—Material Realm _____ Unseen—Spirit Realm
Objective—Principle-Precedent _____ Subjective—Spirit-Led

———

Order: Order:
Fallen Estate _____ Restored Estate
Spirit–spirit Separated _____ Spirits United
Sword Cut Spirit Asunder _____ Sword Circumcision
First Adam's Order _____ Last Adam's Order
Body, Soul, Spirit _____ Spirit, Soul, Body
Courts, Holy, Holiest _____ Holiest, Holy, Courts
Will, Being the: _____ Conscience, Being the:
Law of the Mind/Psyche _____ Law of Spirit/Pneuma
Judgment _____ Righteousness
Line or Horizontal _____ Plummet or Vertical
Birthright or Blessing _____ Blessing and Birthright
King or Priest _____ Priest and King

The first column items are not to be treated as an opposite of the second; rather, the second column items are intrinsically inclusive of the first. The thought being: The first is completed or accomplished in the second.

CHAPTER 4

Biblical Perfection and Overcoming

"Be ye therefore perfect, even as your Father which is in heaven is perfect." (Matthew 5:48)

THE SUBJECT OF "BIBLICAL perfection," correctly understood, will give us added insight into God's plan of the ages. Perfecting the redeemed is the focus of this section. Having the right perspective and attitude will produce neither exaltation nor discouragement. Matthew 5–7 show us the path, conduct, and spirit that Jesus demonstrated. It is God's will that we follow Jesus' example. We are called to emulate Christ's example, especially the beatitudes of Matthew 5:3–11. That would be our "perfection," and only accomplished if we love Him.

Biblical perfection is not doing everything right and without error. "Perfection" must be understood as per "reasonable, scriptural understanding." Otherwise, the matter rest in the rank of the bizarre and unthinkable. Repeating, "perfect" is not saying or doing everything mistake-free.

The intent of this writing will be to gain a confession of heart that the overcoming process is biblical, reasonable, possible, and to be embraced: a God-ordained spiritual operation.

Overcoming sin and perfection is a matter of the heart and disposition. It becomes a reality as we dedicate our life to Christ's teachings and his life example. Jesus' life message is the path we walk. We are called to do both the "hearing" and the "doing" of Christ's example. The "doing" of the thing can only be accomplished as we abide in the "estate of His righteousness" which is imputed to us. In 2Corinthians 5:21, it states, *"For he made him to be sin for us, who knew no sin; that we might be made the righteousness of God in him."*

This section aims to demonstrate, at least in the mind's eye, the construction of a spiritual altar whereby we are effectually "in Christ" and yoked with Christ in the plan of overcoming unto perfection. *"God is the LORD, which hath shewed us light: bind the sacrifice with cords, even unto the horns of the altar"* (Psalms 118:27). That very altar speaks of the sacrificial life. Dying to the Adamic, we are made alive in Christ. To wit: Our God given "vision." Jude 3 calls it *"the common salvation"* and *"the faith"* for which we are to contend.

Approaching this subject, we need to know that God has a plan. The ending state of creation, relating to God's plan, is the final judgment of heaven and earth. Going forward, there remains only the perfected. That is the God-ordained *"new heaven and a new earth"* (Revelation 21:1). Jesus Christ is our God-given example of the citizen of that world to come, a world wherein dwelleth righteousness. Thus, he is the beginning and the end of the subject of perfection. This is our vision: *"the faith."*

There are many aspects to overcoming and perfection. This writing will enumerate and then discuss the necessary introduction of several God-given dispensing and helps toward the perfecting of his children.

This writing is not an easy read. Patience and discipline will yield great reward. Jesus made a related, even applicable statement, in the sense of engagement, determination, and taking care of business: *"For the children of this world are in their generation wiser than the children of light"* (Luke 16:8).

Let it be said regarding the Children of God; due application is given to the task at hand with zeal and a yea, yea spirit complementary to the great Plan of God.*

* Let it be refreshed; this writer does not presume to have a total knowledge of the several precepts discussed, especially perfection. In fact, the presumption of having exhausted the expression of godly precepts, however learned the expositor, touches a root concern of this writer.

Perfection and Unity
"Let Us Go On unto Perfection"

The Plan of God, his *"Word,"* his *"intent,"* is the heartbeat of the Gospel of Jesus Christ. Jesus fulfilled all things, so that he is the *"Word."* The Creation and Creatures are predestined to gain eternal, perfect unity with the Creator. Jesus has that unity with the Father. Jesus gave his life to accomplish, for us, that same at-one-ment, so that he is our atonement. The finish of God's plan will see his goal accomplished unto perfection. That is God's *"intent."* Again, it is his *"Word,"* and *"the mother of us all"* (John 1:1 and Galatians 4:26). Rest in this confidence: all things are of, by, and for Christ. All that continues as eternal will be on the foundation of Christ's prophesied advent, life, death, and resurrection. That being accomplished, we experience Christ's life, sacrifice, and resurrection as God's provision for our reconciliation, perfecting, resurrection, and eternal life. The Lord Jesus Christ is alpha and omega. Jesus has made our calling possible, as we abide "in him." Jesus is God's *"Word"* personified. He is the only *"door,"* or atonement.

Hebrews 6:1–3—*"THEREFORE leaving the principles of the doctrine of Christ, <u>let us go on unto perfection</u>; not laying again the foundation of repentance from dead works, and of faith toward God, 2. Of the doctrine of <u>baptisms</u>, and of <u>laying on of hands</u>, and of <u>resurrection of the dead</u>, and of <u>eternal judgment</u>. 3. And this will we do, if God permit."*

This vertical list connects the doctrines mentioned to the subjects underlined, <u>which are the aspects going forward.</u>

<u>"baptisms"</u>	<u>"laying on of hands"</u>	<u>"resurrection of the dead"</u>	<u>"eternal judgment"</u>

Perfection	Fivefold Ministry	Bride Message	Pathway of Charity
Goal	Government	Product	Foundation

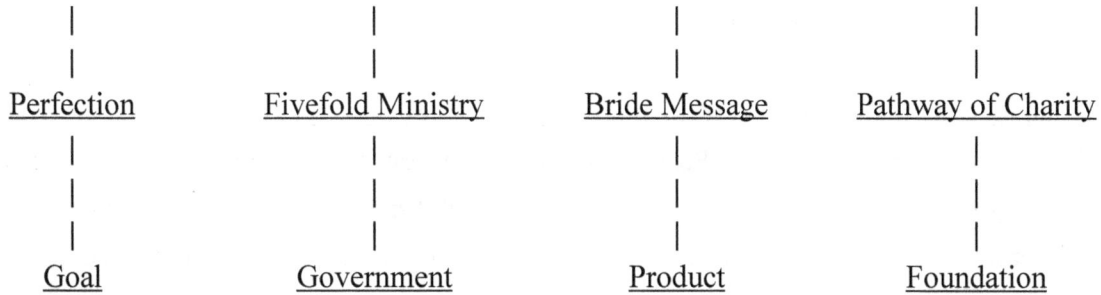

The four <u>doctrines</u> shown laterally across the page are *baptisms, laying on of hands, resurrection of the dead,* and *eternal judgment.* The related four <u>subjects</u> are listed on the line below. They are the four going-on-to-perfection <u>teachings</u>. To wit: *Perfection, Fivefold Ministry, Bride Message,* and *Pathway of Charity.* These four teachings constitute the vital and precious knowledge peculiar to Christ's body of believers. As depicted on the third line of the chart, we gain that "higher ground," God's ordained *"intent"*: the goal, the government, the product, and all on the foundation of loving God, his people, and loving his creation. The heartbeat of this knowledge is the Holy Spirit-implemented going-on which is our calling. The four horns of the altar are often brought forth as a fitting similitude: obedient and committed, as securely tied, because we love God with all our heart, mind, and strength.

The Body of Christ must teach and preach perfection, a fivefold ministry, the Bride message, and the pathway of charity. These may be seen as *"for the perfecting of the saints"* and the *"effectual working"* of Hebrews 6:1–3 above, and Ephesians 4:12, 16. *"For the perfecting of the saints, for the work of the ministry, for the edifying of the body of Christ . . . From whom the whole body fitly joined together and compacted by that which every joint supplieth, according to the effectual working in the measure of every part, maketh increase of the body unto the edifying of itself in love."*

<u>Baptisms</u>: Fully realized and implemented, this doctrine nets <u>perfection</u>. A primary thought and principle in baptisms is that we are restored and not reformed. The Lord requires that *"old things are passed away"* and *"all things are become new"* (2 Corinthians 5:17). That is, a death to the flesh life, a death to the carnal mind, will, and emotions, and a rebirth in the Spirit which is of God. Polishing up the fallen Adam is not God's plan, not soulish but Spirit.

<u>Laying on of hands</u>: This doctrine, going forward, gives us the <u>officiating or government of the Body</u>, which doctrine is necessary for the perfecting of the Saints: More "officiating" of the ministry and less structure or organization. Hebrews 11:40 declares, *"They without us (fivefold ministry) should not be made perfect."*

<u>Resurrection of the dead</u>: This doctrine embraces the <u>Bride message</u> and gives us the second witness (144,000) of the high-water mark resurrection of Christ. The resurrection doctrine cannot be explained without the God-given revelation on this doctrine. Lacking this understanding, the message becomes unlikely and even bizarre. <u>The "Bride message" is where the goal of perfection is best preached and understood.</u> It is here that the second witness, the Very Elect (Bride), will testify, as did Jesus, that *"The prince of this world cometh, and hath nothing in me"* (John 14:30). For further explanation, see Chapter VI.

Note: The "man child . . . *caught up unto God, and to his throne*" (Revelation 12:5), is the same as the returning "bride, *the Lamb's wife*" (Revelation 21:9); returning after 1,000 years transpire.

Eternal judgment: The doctrinal truth and message on the pathway of charity is like the pearl of great price hidden in the grand doctrine of Eternal Judgment. The very foundation of his Body and the totality of God's plan is that *"God so loved the world, that he gave his only begotten Son"* (John 3:16). This being accomplished, Jesus Christ set in motion the continuance (eternally) of all things that please God, and causes to perish (eternally) all things that offend. That is the eternal and concluding end. Thus, it is the course or plan of *"eternal judgment."* Jesus said, Matthew 16:18, *"Upon this rock I will build my church."* Truly it is our foundation and operating system. Christ's judgment in our lives moves us on to perfection. Most important is the fact that the whole of the matter is founded and flavored with his Love.

The Church embraces a goal (perfection), a government (fivefold ministry), a product (man child/bride), and a foundation (pathway of charity).

Perfect: The Word
(Let Us Review the Premises)

Jesus said, *"Be ye therefore perfect, even as your Father which is in heaven is perfect"* (Matthew 5:48). The word "perfect" expresses the concept of being "complete," even "finished." The same Greek word is used in James 1:4, *"But let patience have her perfect work, that ye may be perfect and entire, wanting nothing."* Also, Ephesians 4:13, *"Till we all come in the unity of the faith, and of the knowledge of the Son of God, unto a perfect man, unto the measure of the stature of the fullness of Christ."*

Perfection is mistakenly viewed as doing everything right, having total maturity, and never missing the mark. This perception of perfection would lead a person toward will worship and a very human "works" mentality. "Perfection" is often approached from the standpoint of our doings, our definitions. and our perceptions. The tragedy of this emphasis is that we might settle for a pride-driven corral, or trap, where the natural mind rides around in circles. Then, the confession comes forth: It is impossible! Consequently, much of Christendom marginalizes or outright rejects the biblical message of perfection as unattainable. That is reasonably true, but Jesus stated a principle: *"With men this is impossible; but with God all things are possible"* (Matthew 19:26).

Perfection pertains to the dispositional part, where his Spirit connects and works in our spirit. It is a spiritual work and the *determinations*, or doing of the thing, is God working "in us," and us "in Him." Rest assured; his Glory, not ours, His righteousness, not ours. *"For as many as are led by the Spirit of God, they are the sons of God"* (Romans 8:14).

Perfection: The Subject

This biblical imperative is typically treated from the standpoint of an individual "striving" for the sinless life, purity of mind and body, and maturity. Humbly stated: We must understand that on a platform of truth, "our striving" cannot entertain contest or emulation, especially relating to our fellow believers. Referring expressly to that point: Philippians 1:27 states, *"Stand fast in one spirit, with one mind, <u>striving together</u> for the faith of the gospel."* The meaning of *"strive"* in the native idiom (Greek), as used in this Scripture, is to endeavor and struggle, even <u>agonize together</u>. Correctly defined, we believe that to strive for perfection is good and correct.

Having this charity evident among us, we progress with carefulness; not stopping our progress in God with "reconciliation," but going forward we spiritually embrace his "life example," which is our "pathway of charity." *"For if, when we were enemies, we were <u>reconciled</u> to God by the death of his Son, <u>much more</u>, being reconciled, we shall be saved by <u>his life</u>"* (Romans 5:10). To be reconciled and converted equates to a place "in him." It is the place in God where the ongoing work of at-one-ment and perfection continues. Conversion and reconciliation are essentially our entrance "into Christ," the very estate or spiritual habitation where we grow in Christ. It is another expression for experiencing a growth of the inner man. Made possible because of *"Christ in you, the hope of glory"* (Colossians 2:27).

A sinless life lies in a total and complete embrace of the Lord's exemplary life. That is an operation of Holy Ghost power in the inner man, taking on his nature. *"Whereby are given unto us exceeding great and precious promises: that by these ye might be <u>partakers of the divine nature</u>, having escaped the corruption that is in the world through lust"* (2 Peter 1:4).

The course of overcoming deals with all sin; weights, conduct, manners, deportment, demeanor, and conversation. In the overview; overcoming is realizing spiritual dominion and the defeat of our otherwise pride-driven life with its works of the flesh. *"Adultery, fornication, uncleanness, lasciviousness, Idolatry, witchcraft, hatred, variance, emulation, wrath, strife, seditions, heresies, Envying, murders, drunkenness, revellings, and such like"* (Galatians 5:19–21); traits of the carnal mind, will, and emotions. Those things are typical to fallen man and his pride-driven nature.

Perfection is a more profound inner work that sees the *carnal nature*, or disposition of the Adamic, die and the nature of Christ made manifest. That is, him in us and us in him. Stated in biblical terms: *"For whom he did foreknow, he also did predestinate to be conformed to the image of his Son, that he might be the firstborn among many brethren"* (Romans 8:29).

Perfection: Thy Will Be Done

Perfecting (perfection) our embrace of Jesus leaves no place for a "willful" route to greatness. Perish the thought that such an embrace would accommodate even the desire for a status of infallibility; the high-water mark of a prideful status. A great danger lies with our persistence in qualifying and expressing the matter of perfection as though it resides in the court of "<u>our</u> will be done." We risk discounting the *"power"* mentioned in Acts 1:8. *"Ye shall receive power, after that the Holy Ghost is come upon you."* That equates to "<u>thy</u> *will be done."*

Our submitted will is good and the application of our will is required. However, the grace-given Spiritual Power is where the perfecting is wrought in the life of a Holy Ghost person. *"And ye are complete in him, which is the head of all principality and power"* (Colossians 2:10). This is the "best." The "good," our submitted will, would be counterproductive to the "best" if it becomes a stopping point. The best is dispensed from heaven. Quoting again, Jesus said *"Ye shall receive power, after that the Holy Ghost is come upon you"* (Acts 1:8). We must reckon our willful striving as being subordinate to the spiritual operation of the Holy Ghost; let the flavor of that be "patience" as we rest in our faith in him. That operation is accomplished in the spiritual arena of our quickened conscience, communion, and intuition.

The *"power"* (Acts 1:8), in terms of the scriptural imperative; was given to spread the Gospel, good news, to the unsaved. Jesus said, *"Let your light so shine before men, that they may see your good works, and glorify your Father which is in heaven"* (Matthew 5:16).

Romans 7 gives an account of the limited result of a willful obedience to the Law, yielding no change of *disposition* (our heart or spirit) and failing to accomplish God's perfect will.

Reading into chapter 8, we understand that being *"in Christ Jesus"* (Romans 8:1) embraces the operation of the Spirit. Holy Ghost power gains us freedom and dominion over *"the law of sin and death"* (Romans 8:2). The prospect of *"go on unto perfection"* (Hebrews 6:1) is not of the Law, it is of Grace; that is, being *"in Christ Jesus."*

The accomplishing of God's perfect will in the lives of his Saints, and the Church collectively, is not per-our-will. It is per-His-Will. Outside the "In Christ," Holy Ghost estate, even a submitted will, *"the law of the mind"* (Romans 7:23), is no match for the *"law of sin and death"* (Romans 8:2). The actual doing of God's will is a spiritual matter; so that, it must be facilitated and made possible thru the operation of the Holy Ghost, the Spirit of God reunited with the spirit in man. This allows for the Holy Ghost to effectually work in the life of a Saint of God. To be born-again of the Spirit, to become a Child of God, in Christ, a New Creature; that is the Grace of God. It is the estate of his imputing the righteousness of Christ in us and not imputing our sins. It is God's will that His Grace result in the perfecting of the Saints.

To deny the message of overcoming and perfection is to deny God's will and the divine operation of His Grace in our lives.

Knowing these things, we are sure that <u>our striving</u> must not be a matter of willful determinations, rather, according as <u>our will is submitted to God's Holy Spirit Power</u>. That power ministers to us as being born-again and living our lives under the blood of Christ and "in Christ." The comparable "estate" would be "in the world but not of the world." An awareness, confession, and submission of our will to God's will help us better grasp and embrace the scriptural path of overcoming and perfection. Being in spiritual order moves us toward a "complete" embrace of Christ's example. To be completely "in Christ" is tantamount to being completed/perfected. The new man has replaced the old man.

Perfection: God's Predetermined Will

The apostle Paul gives a key statement of understanding: *"And we know that all things work together for good to them that love God, to them who are the called according to his purpose. For whom he did foreknow, he also did predestinate to be conformed to the image of his Son, that he might be the firstborn among many brethren. Moreover whom he did predestinate, them he also called: and whom he called, them he also justified: and whom he justified, them he also glorified"* (Romans 8:28–30).

The message of perfection and overcoming is very much an ingredient in God's predetermined plan. As pertaining to us, this is the Grace of God, and the Glory of God. The message of perfection is in God's court in a fashion that subjugates our handling of the matter. The accomplishing of his will and his plan in our lives is that we be made perfect. And that is the Lord's provision. Therein lies the working of the Holy Spirit and mediation. The Father's supply of Grace, as per his predestined will, constituting our course, which yields the desired overcoming transformation.

Pertaining to our part, Romans 9:16 states, *"So then it is not of him that willeth, nor of him that runneth, but of God that sheweth mercy."* We *"willeth,"* we *"runneth,"* but it is *"of God that sheweth mercy."* (Please note that this statement is made in the context of God's predetermined will.) All pertaining to the Lord's provision also applies to the Saints collectively, the Church; *"A glorious church, not having spot, or wrinkle, or any such thing; but that it should be holy and without blemish"* (Ephesians 6:27).

On that point: Jesus paid all, but we do likewise according to his example, as being *"conformed to the image of his Son"* (Romans 8:20).

Perfection: The Spirit Is Where the Change Happens

It is God's Spirit working in the spirit of man that leads us on the path toward perfection. That reflects our at-one-ment with God thru Christ. His shed blood is the price of our purchase, so that he is the atonement. Our purchase can be termed "our atonement." That is, our at-one-ment or Spirit–spirit reconnection. Jesus is the *"door"* (John 10:1–9). Jesus is the *"true vine, and my Father is the husbandman"* (John 15:1). This similitude speaks not only to the life in the vine, but the growth that is inherently in the vine, the production of fruit. That is God's intent, and it is His Plan for us. Who would resist? Only a fool or those gaining entry as thieves and robbers; and, how could that be accomplished under God's purview?

The work is of God. Perfection is an ongoing operation of the Spirit. Again, there must be a reconnection of man's spirit with God, who is Spirit. *"For as many as are led by the Spirit of God, they are the sons of God. For ye have not received the spirit of bondage again to fear; but ye have received the Spirit of adoption, whereby we cry, Abba, Father. The Spirit itself beareth witness with our spirit, that we are the children of God"* (Romans 8:14–16).

Receiving the Holy Ghost is the event of reconnection of man's spirit with God's Spirit. God is Spirit, and the event is a birth unto "sonship." Adam forfeited that relationship.

On the point of *"led by the Spirit of God"*: We are led by the Spirit–spirit connection in matters pertaining to the victories we experience in our trials and testing. With Adam, it pertained to dominion over the creation. With us, it matters greatly that we gain personal dominion relating to the wiles of the flesh, the devil, and the world; spiritual dominion. Scriptural references are manifold. Rest assured, it is the message of the New Testament. Reconciliation and our perfecting happen in this auspice. It is God's court and Jesus is Lord and Mediator. The Holy Ghost is facilitator.

As saith the Scripture, *"Yea, though we have known Christ after the flesh, yet now henceforth know we him no more. Therefore if any man be in Christ, he is a* <u>*new creature*</u>: *old things are passed away; behold, all things are become new. And all things are of God, who hath reconciled us to himself by Jesus Christ, and hath given to us the ministry of reconciliation"* (2 Corinthians 5:16–18). It is a spiritual work that inherently relates to *"a new creature"* and not a reformed old man, or *"old things."* It is about dying to the flesh. *"For if ye live after the flesh, ye shall die: but if ye through the Spirit do mortify the deeds of the body, ye shall live"* (Romans 8:13). The work is of God and it is of the Holy Ghost and spiritual.

Reckoning yourself dead is akin to being alive in Christ; that would be the *"*<u>*new creature,*</u>*"* and death to the old man Adam. Overcoming is dying to the old man and eventually giving way to the completed *"*<u>*new creature.*</u>*"* Anything less will fall into the category of a reformed old man. God's plan is restoration; that is, a new creature, not refitting and polishing up the old man.

Scripturally understood, *perfection* is God's work of redemption ongoing and finally *"finished"* (John 17:4), in the Lord's Body of Believers, all by his life's example. Made possible by his shed blood, *"finished"* (John 19:30). Always and without fail, perfection happens because Christ gave his life. And, his righteousness indwells our lives. And, because we are servant-like, submitted in brokenness, with humility and thankfulness, he delights to reckon our at-one-ment. He is our atonement. That equates to the oneness of Spirit–spirit.

God's Will and Means in the Matter of "Let Us Go On unto Perfection"

Ministries, however spirit-led and inspiring, will not increase the inner man. The spirit in man is impacted by the power of the Holy Ghost, and the Spirit of God acts and leads us from the inside. That is not psyche, but pneuma power. The inner man is the *"Christ in you,"* born in us by Spirit birth. Only the indwelling Holy Ghost working effectually will change the heart of man. That is the means to the end of what God's intends for us, a permanent change of heart.

The initialization LLL is a good memory peg to bring to mind the Holy Ghost quickening of God's <u>Love</u>, God's <u>Learning</u>, and God's <u>Leading</u> in the spirit of a born-again child of God. The reason being:

<u>The gift of the Holy Ghost is the rejoining of man's spirit to God's Spirit.</u> *"But he that is joined unto the Lord is one spirit"* (1 Corinthians 6:17). The Holy Ghost is the facilitator. How else could the works of God be accomplished in the spirit of man? That is, in the inner man. Again, how else but *"Christ in you, the hope of glory"* (Colossians 1:27). And, *"Having begun in the Spirit, are ye now made perfect by the flesh?"* (Galatians 3:3).

The operation of the gift of the Holy Ghost will both reveal and increase Love, Learning, and Leading; *"Unto a perfect man, unto the measure of the stature of the fullness of Christ"* (Ephesians 4:13). The perfecting of love, learning, and leading is foundational in the *"perfecting of the Saints"* (verse 12). (Regarding the context: Gifted men of God minister as Holy Ghost operatives.) Another Scripture that reflects the Spirit–spirit reality is Romans 8:15, 16; *"For ye have not received the spirit of bondage again to fear; but ye received the Spirit of adoption, whereby we cry, Abba, Father. The Spirit itself beareth witness with our spirit, that we are the children of God."*

Following are features and Scriptures relating to the Holy Ghost's operation:

Chart

Love of God	Learn of God	Led of God
Son-ship	Vision	Anointing
Christ-like	Change	Mandate
Sacrificial	Increase	Dominion
Holy/Harmless	Peace/Freedom	Obedience/Power
Romans 5:5	John 14:26	Romans 8:14

Love: Romans 5:5—*"The love of God is shed abroad in our hearts by the Holy Ghost which is given unto us."*

Learn: John 14:26—*"But the Comforter, which is the Holy Ghost, whom the Father will send in my name, he shall teach you all things, and bring all things to your remembrance, whatsoever I have said unto you."*

Led: Romans 8:14—*"For as many as are led by the Spirit of God, they are the sons of God."*

Jesus' Example Shows Us a Finished Product

Romans 5:1–11 demonstrates the mandate to continue our progress in Christ. The eleven verses are "rightly divided" as a profit to our understanding and to amplify on the thought of *"go on unto perfection,"* as stated in Hebrews 6:1. To wit: Not stopping or leveling off at any point in God's plan for our lives. That is the will of God. He desires a "finished" product. Again, this text in Romans 5 helps make that point. The addition of underlining and bold type is not meant to add to or take away, but rather to clarify.

The italicized Scripture quotes refer to the *"reconciliation"* aspect, as understood and agreed to by most of Christianity.

The italicized Scripture quotes in bold type, will refer to the ***"let us go on to perfection"*** aspect.

Romans 5:1–11—*1." Therefore being justified by faith, we have peace with God through our Lord Jesus Christ: 2. By whom also we have access by faith into this grace wherein we stand, and rejoice in hope of the glory of God.*

*3. And not only so, **but we glory in tribulations also: knowing that tribulation worketh patience; 4. And patience, experience; and experience, hope: 5. And hope maketh not ashamed; because the love of God is shed abroad in our hearts by the Holy Ghost which is given unto us.***

6. Underline(For) when we were yet without strength, in due time Christ died for the ungodly. 7. For scarcely for a righteous man will one die: yet peradventure for a good man some would even dare to die. 8. But God commendeth his love toward us, in that, while we were yet sinners, Christ died for us.

*9. Much more then, being now justified by his blood, **we shall be saved from wrath through him.***

10. For if, when we were enemies, we were reconciled to God by the death of his Son,

*much more, **being reconciled, we shall be saved by his life. 11. And not only so, but we also joy in God through our Lord Jesus Christ, by whom we have now received the atonement.***"

Note: The discussion of "perfection" makes mention of "estate" or "place in God." The reason being: by God's Grace we are entered into the going-on or growing up *"unto a perfect man, unto the measure of the stature of the fullness of Christ"* (Ephesians 4:13). The Church is such an "estate" or place. The following sections are introduced as a help to see the significance of the Church in God's plan relating to our perfection and eternal salvation. As such, the Church is to be embraced as a second heaven operation. The Church is a mystery, but it is not mystical. The Church is a literal observable entity.

Perfection: The Church Has an Integral Part

The Church is spoken of, in similitude, as Christ' wife. *"For the husband is the head of the wife, even as Christ is the head of the church: and he is the savior of the body. Therefore as the church is subject unto Christ, so let the wives be to their own husbands in every thing. Husbands, love your wives, even as Christ also loved the church, and gave himself for it"* (Ephesians 5:23–25). The apostle Paul made a further statement: *"I am jealous over you with godly jealousy: for I have espoused you to one husband, that I may present you as a chaste virgin to Christ"* (2 Corinthians 11:2).

Revelation 12:1, 2, and 5 speaks of the woman, the Church of which Christ is the head, that brings forth the high-water mark product of the two-thousand-year church age. To wit: *"A woman clothed with the sun, and the moon under her feet, and upon her head a crown of twelve stars: And she being with child cried, travailing in birth, and pained to be delivered . . . And she brought forth a man child, who was to rule all nations with a rod of iron: and her child was caught up unto God, and to his throne."**

Ideally, the Church has, or will, in a more perfect sense, gain the realm of *"in heavenly places in Christ Jesus"* (Ephesians 2:6). That being the case, we would have a spiritual estate present in the Church, being in similitude, the Holy Place. Godly ministries officiate in this heavenly realm. Ministers of God that are Holy Ghost operatives, having this testimony: *"The testimony of Jesus is the spirit of prophecy"* (Revelation 19:10). If the word of God is preached in Spirit and Truth, rest assured, it is heaven connected, spiritual and prophetic. There will be present spiritual manna, spiritual light, and the sweet savor of heaven-connected prayer and worship. It is a Holy Place operation.**

This Church, of which Christ is the head, has a mother, and that mother is *"Jerusalem which is above is free, which is the mother of us all"* (Galatians 4:26). This is a precious truth and *"hard to be understood."* The Church portrays the very plan and intent of God. The *"mother"* of the whole creation and human chronicle is God's plan, his will, his *"Word"*; Jesus, the personification.

God's *"Word"* was manifest at the advent of Jesus birth and life, *"The Word was made flesh, and dwelt among us"* (John 1:14). Likewise, the mystery of the more completed plan will be revealed; finally, manifest on earth. See Revelation 21:10, *"And he carried me away in the spirit to a great and high mountain, and shewed me that great city, the holy Jerusalem, descending out of heaven from God."*

It is the Grace of God, his great Love manifest, that we have a unity with Jesus and the vision. All because the Spirit–spirit connection, *"in Christ,"* abides. Thus, our name is written in heaven and our place in the Church is assured. It is his body of believers. The perfecting of the Saints is integral to his plan, which is the *"Word"* of God.

The Church is established primarily by the Apostle. He is in harmony with the Master Builder which is Christ. Such, the Apostle is builder and, if needs be, also Evangelist and Teacher. He carries the burden of unifying the people, as would the later ordained resident Pastor. The Church; the *ecclesia*, is a body of believers united in purpose and vision. The Apostle causes to be instilled in the operation, a judgment factor. That would be a people giving the light of Love and Righteousness and Service: servant-like, charitable, and sacrificial. The Church members' lives are light and judgment by example, more than mere words. The Apostle's office pertains to laying the foundation of Christ' order, truth, and vision. His office is impossible by human standards. Only the Holy Ghost's *"unction"* will move the perfecting of the Church toward its end. The end being a precious collective of like-minded Saints. *"A city that is set on a hill cannot be hid"* (Matthew 5:14).

A resident Apostle would be desired, but that presence is sometimes registered only as the continuing spiritual effect of his anointed planting and teachings. Ordained local ministers take up the cause in his absence.

If the continuing burden of the Apostle is the unity of the people, even so, the continuing burden of the Prophet is that the people be in unity with the Lord above. The Prophet prioritizes and ministers the third heaven-connection. More than the apparent order, unity, and teaching, it is the "spirit" of the church operation. More particularly, the "spirit of the vision." This imparting and partaking is established and resides as the work of the Prophet. Like the Apostle, his presence is necessary and solicited. But, like the Apostle, he will likely not be a continuing presence, as he travels to other needed places. Necessarily, the *"the testimony of Jesus . . . the spirit of prophecy"* continues in the Church (Revelation 19:10).

The Church, to wit: *"But ye are come unto mount Sion, and unto the city of the living God, the heavenly Jerusalem, and to an innumerable company of angels, To the general assembly and church of the firstborn, which are written in heaven, and to God the Judge of all, and to the spirits of just men made perfect, And to Jesus the mediator of the new covenant, and to the blood of sprinkling, that speaketh better things than that of Abel"* (Hebrews 12:22–24). More than just being the righteous line, the Church is of the faith of Abraham and the Sons of God. The Church is Family.

Some term the Church, our "extended family." Others say, our "second family." That integrates well with the following section. Call it our "second heaven family."

* The more accepted interpretation of Revelation 12:1–6 is that the *"woman"* is Israel and the nation brings forth Jesus as savior. However, naturally, the righteous line thru David brought forth Christ and God was his father. Also, during Jesus' lifetime till his Ascension, Israel did not stand on the moon (Law), nor was the nation clothed in the sun (Grace).

** We do not know how the Church will eventually be structured, logistics wise, because of future restraints and persecutions. Some predict an underground church operation in days to come. Likely, it will evolve quickly and then do its sacrificial work in a "short season," as a unified ecclesia's martyrs' death; figurative for most and literal for some. Going forward, the remnant will transition to a millennium format.

The Second Heaven Estate, As Pertaining to the Church

The term *second heaven* is not mentioned explicitly in Scripture. However, the term is brought forward here because of scriptural references to *"first"* and *"third"* heaven: *First heaven* is mentioned repeatedly in Scripture. In 2 Corinthians 12:2, Paul speaks of being *"caught up to the third heaven."* If first and third are referenced, where is second? The Church is such an estate. The Church is not mystical, but it is a mystery; and, understanding the church operation is a mystery revealed.

(Jesus' advent was a revealing of the "mystery," and, Jesus being *"the head of the body, the church"* (Colossians 1:18), we are further benefited as we embrace the Church of which he is the head.)

Relating to physical parameters, it is sort of a moot question. It is hardly a consideration in this writing, and further suppositions are not treated. Events, as we perceive them, are ongoing and they are in the observable and psychological realms. That is, all explained in the context of this physical habitation. Second heaven addresses restoration and the overturning of evil. That operation is spiritual in basis. However observable, it is heavenly propagated.

The term *second*, as attached to <u>heaven</u>, deserves consideration because it is part of rightly understanding and explaining God's word. The word *second* can denote witness, judgment, overturning, and restoration, especially as it relates to order.

Hebrews 10:9 states; *"He taketh away the <u>first</u>, that he may establish the <u>second</u>."* We understand this transition from the Law to Grace, but Grace is the very object of the chapter, including the Church, which is the God-ordained second heaven we are blessed to occupy.

In 1 Corinthians 15:47, it states; *"The <u>first man</u> is of the earth, earthy: the <u>second man</u> is the Lord from heaven."* By faith we embrace Jesus Christ. He is that <u>second</u> man who has authored our present spiritual <u>second</u> heaven state.

Presently, second heaven is a spiritual place in Christ, having a third heaven reconnection. In time, it will become a literal reality; a theocratic kingdom. That will be *"a new heaven and a new earth"* (Revelation 21:1).

Obviously, we reside in first heaven, but we do embrace the heavenly vision. A good similitude is the Tabernacle in the wilderness. It was pitched on typical desert terrain, but inside the 50 x 100 cubits was a different world: It was the picture of salvation pertaining to the heavenly vision. To wit: In the world but not of the world.

Again, second heaven is a spiritual condition: the Church, the Body of Christ. Again, it is in similitude, a tabernacle in the wilderness; it is the saved, reflecting salvation and sanctification, tabernacling in a temporal world; whereby we are ordained to forsake a carnal life of *"the lust of the flesh, and the lust of the eyes, and the pride of life"* (1 John 2:16). We are dedicated to the heavenly vision. See 2 Corinthians 6:16–18.

The new heaven of Revelation 21:1 is future; so, presently, the literal new or second heaven is experienced only by faith. Herein lies a precious truth. To wit: Those *"in Christ"* have, by faith, entered into, or at least embraced, a second heaven condition. Paul states in Ephesians 2:6, *"And hath raised us up together, and made us sit together in heavenly places in Christ Jesus."* All made possible by the shed blood of Jesus and the coming into being of the Church on the day of Pentecost.

Consider 2 Corinthians 5:17, *"New creature . . . behold, all things are become new."* Not only transition from the Law to Grace but, in the overview, this newness is foundational to the New Testament message. This is *"The kingdom of heaven"* message spoken of by Jesus in Matthew 10:7; and, furthermore, knowing that in the final restitution and *"the redemption of the purchased possession"* we will no longer *"groan within ourselves, waiting for the adoption, to wit, the redemption of our body"* (Ephesians 1:14, Romans 8:23). Also verse 22, *"Know that the whole creation groaneth and travaileth in pain together until now."* This is our *"hope"* and our *"rejoicing"* (Romans 8:24, 12:12).

Perfection: The Ministry of the Church Is a Necessary Part

The apostle Paul told the Church at Ephesus that the gifts of ministry were for the perfecting of the saints. *"And he gave some, apostles; and some, prophets; and some, evangelist; and some, pastors and teachers; For the perfecting of the saints, for the work of the ministry, for the edifying of the body of Christ: Till we all come in the unity of the faith, and of the knowledge of the Son of God, unto a perfect man, unto the measure of the stature of the fullness of Christ"* (Ephesians 4:11–13).

Overcoming and perfecting are mostly in the area of mind, will, and emotions. Simply put: That is the soul. That is, you: the person. This is where the fire burns. Consider Pentecost, they were initiates into the Baptism of Fire. That reflection is ongoing. It is God-ordained, and, it is the Lord's provision. It is good that we respond to the soul-cleansing ministering of a Holy Ghost kind. It is for our perfecting. As do clean animals; per similitude, we eat, bring up, and rechew our first ingestion; that is, <u>firstly</u>, we read or hear a truth and reasonably assimilate the thing in our mind. Necessarily, the first partaking is spirit-inspired, both in the administering and on the part of the partaker. That would be a "Holy Place" experience. The burden of the Teacher-gift would be that the hearer or reader does partake and assimilate. The burden of the Pastor-gift is that the recipients be *"doers"* (James 1:22). Then, <u>secondly</u>, the matter is revisited as *"praying in the Holy Ghost"*

(Jude 20). That is a "Holiest Place" experience where *The Spirit itself beareth witness with our spirit, that we are the children of God"* (Romans 8:16).

The apostle Paul held to the vision that he received and shared as an ambassador for Christ. *"Now then we are ambassadors for Christ, as though God did beseech you by us: we pray you in Christ's stead, be ye reconciled to God"* (2 Corinthians 5:20). A gifted minister is spirit-led, speaking the plan and will of God to the Church. That is, speaking as a Holy Ghost operative and manifesting the Word of God, promoting the message of perfection. How can it be otherwise unless God's Plan, Will, and Operation of Grace are less than perfect? No, God and all that pertains to the Plan, the Word, *"the mother of us all,"* is perfect. In similar fashion, the Church is to be *"a glorious church, not having spot, or wrinkle, or any such thing; but that it should be holy and without blemish"* (Ephesians 5:27).

The true ministry knows that the effectual doing of the thing is that their attendees spend time in spiritual communion. So that their first ingestion is refreshed, in brokenness, and become assimilated in their spirit. With intercessory prayer and meditation, in the Spirit–spirit connection, we gain the Holiest Place experience. That similitude reflects our Spirit–spirit life. There is where the change comes. The perfecting change, growing the *"new creature,"* a personal, spiritual event. That is essentially the pith and marrow of the similitude of chewing the cud. Without the needed step past the Holy Place to the Holiest we may, in the worst case, be *"having a form of godliness, but denying the power thereof . . . Ever learning, and never able to come to the knowledge of the truth"* (2 Timothy 3:5, 7).

In Jude 20, we read this statement, *"But ye, beloved, building up yourselves on your most holy faith, praying in the Holy Ghost."* Prayer to what end? We do not always know. Sometimes, our intercessory prayer, in the Holy Ghost, relates directly to a recently inspired reading or lesson from the ministry, or, at other times, not so. The ministry, within the Church scenario or not, needs to reinforce this understanding with their attendees.

Romans 8:26–29 speaks volumes on that particular point of understanding. *"Likewise the Spirit also helpeth our infirmities: for we know not what we should pray for as we ought: but the Spirit itself maketh intercession for us with groanings which cannot be uttered. And he that searcheth the hearts knoweth what is the mind of the Spirit, because he maketh intercession for the saints according to the will of God. And we know that all things work together for good to them that love God, to them who are the called according to his purpose. For whom he did foreknow, he also did predestinate to be conformed to the image of his Son, that he might be the firstborn among many brethren."*

The spiritual progress of God's people towards perfection will not stop with men's administration, however necessary and however great in our eyes. Getting our eyes set on man's ability is unfair to those men of God and it frustrates the perfect will of God for the Church. The Holy Spirit ministering through a gifted person is effectual toward the Church because of Holy Ghost-facilitated spiritual hearing and spiritual vision. It is *"the testimony of Jesus . . . the Spirit of Prophecy"* (Revelation 19:10), which is the connecting link, and that is to the glory of God, not men.

We love, honor, and, in many ways, revere the present ministry. That is good. However, above all, worship God and hold the Lord in his place as Mediator, and no other, dreading, lest any would build unto themselves.

Chart Representation: Fivefold Ministry and Gifts

The Ministry is integral to the Plan of the *"restitution of all things."* This chart reflects that part which is necessary in matters of *"the perfecting of the saints."* The eleven items are worthy of serious contemplation. They address the functional aspect *"of laying on of hands."*

This relates to godly government: "ordained officiation," not structure.

Following are thoughts and compared items with respect to the Gifts of the Ministry to the Church. No item listed is exclusive to a particular gift. All are integrated and inclusive with respect to abilities, functions, and consequences. The items listed under the gift heading only highlight the character and features that are most likely peculiar to that particular gift. In the overview, this chart gives the Saints cause for expectations and dedications relating to the Ministry.

	Apostle	Prophet	Teacher	Pastor	Evangelist
Senses:	Feeling	Seeing	Hearing	Tasting	Smelling
Hand:	Thumb	Index Finger	Tall Finger	Fourth Finger	Fifth Finger
Acting As:	Strong	Resolute	Patient	Fearless	Hopeful
Burden:	Division	Enmity	Unbelief	Disobedience	Prejudice
Calling:	Unity among Men	Unity with God	Faith Believing	Obedience	Accepting
As per:	Line or Judgment	Plummet or Righteousness	Up from the Foundation	Increase of Conscience	Desire for Kingdom
Work:	Foundation	Direction	Product/Goal	Cause/Growth	Zeal/Hope
Nature of:	Build the Garner	Fear God	Hearing	Doing	Cast the Net
Unction:	Conscience	Communion	Leading	Intuition	Sensation

Dealing With:	Body of Believers	Spirit or Pneuma	Soul or Psyche	Baptisms Faithfulness	Entry Envision
	|	|	|	|	|
Like a:	King	Priest	Builder	Ecclesia Garner	Net

Perfection: Its Accomplishment Is a Mystery

The Ministry of the Church speaks of Jesus who was Truth: *"And without controversy great is the mystery of godliness: God was manifest in the flesh, justified in the Spirit, seen of angels, preached unto the Gentiles, believed on in the world, received up into glory"* (1 Timothy 3:16).

A connected thought: It is a mystery. How does rational, thoughtful truth, after being received in our natural minds then refreshed, become a continuing quality of the disposition? That is, our nature is changed toward the fruits of the spirit, displacing the works of the flesh in the disposition: the spiritual part. What we do confess, it is a mystery.

We are born-again of the Spirit, and as Scripture states: *"This mystery . . . which is Christ in you, the hope of glory: Whom we preach, warning every man, and teaching every man in all wisdom; that we may present every man perfect in Christ Jesus"* (Colossians 1:27, 28).

While we lack the innate mental capacity to comprehend the mechanics of Spirit phenomena, the gifts and blessings of the Spirit of God are humbly and gratefully accepted. And that, as a matter of faith, is believing.

Refreshing a related thought: Beyond our comprehension, Jesus effortlessly translated from Spirit to a physical body, then to Spirit, in view of the disciples. There is no science among man that can even imagine the mechanics of that. Nevertheless, how blessed and refreshed we are when we rejoice, in faith believing his glorious victory and divinity. Scripture expresses our end benefit of such faith: *"That he would grant you, according to the riches of his glory, to be strengthened with might by his Spirit in the inner man; That Christ may dwell in your hearts by faith; that ye being rooted and grounded in love, May be able to comprehend with all saints what is the breadth, and length, and depth, and height; And to know the love of Christ, which passeth knowledge, that ye might be filled with all the fullness of God"* (Ephesians 3:16–19).

Perfection: God's Requirement Pertaining to the Bigger Picture

The perfecting of the saints involves the Angelic Host. Hebrews 1:14 states, *"Are they not all ministering spirits, sent forth to minister for them who shall be heirs of salvation?"* The introduction of angelic involvement may be difficult to integrate into the message, but it is very much an ongoing reality. Commensurate with that thought is that the perfecting of individuals and the Church as a Body of Believers is critical in the judgment of this Gentile world. Exemplary lives and a Church without fault are the required standard that will justify the wrath of God ending this present age. That is: Exemplary lives reflecting the works of God, even the sacrifice of their lives. It is to the glory of God when a ministry is completed, *"finished."* On that point; the apostle

Paul was no doubt approaching a fulfilled calling when he said, *"Not as though I had already attained, either were already perfect: but I follow after, if that I may apprehend that for which also I am apprehended of Christ Jesus"* (Philippians 3:12). Paul may have been referring to a *"finished"* ministry, not the "sin factor" and overcoming.

Note: "Overcomer" status has been and will be a reality for the many, maybe millions, in their lifetime before death.*

A question may have entered the readers mind as to limiting perfection and overcoming to a typical life-span; or, is overcoming in the life after resurrection included in the discussion? Yes, "overcomer" status is also realized by the great host that resurrects during the millennium as a terrestrial and completely qualifies for citizenship in the new heaven and new earth. And that is equivalent to "going on to perfection" or overcoming. To see this as a "second chance" misses the mark in terms of truly knowing God's plan. A more complete understanding can be gotten by reading the next chapter on resurrection.

*The 144,000 Very Elect, or *"bride,"* or *"man child"* will be chosen of God from this host of overcomers. This particular *election*, or choosing, is unto a celestial state and immortality. This select 144,000 will be those of the First Resurrection. This understanding will be made clearer in the next chapter on resurrection.

Summation

Perfection is God's will accomplished, or completed, in a life that is servant-like, humbly submitted, and reconciled to his hand on our life. The message of perfection, or overcoming, is paramount and required scripturally. To continue speaking truth on this foundational precept, we need to cease qualifying the doing-of-the-thing as though it is primarily in our hands; rather, place it in God's hands. Our life at his disposal. Simply put: The accomplishing of a perfect Church, individual, or Ministry is more his business than it is ours. His determination, not ours; so that perfection on our part equates to being completely submitted to God's will. Thus, the flavor, in the matter of perfection, is humility. This is a sweet savor, especially in view of the big picture.

Martyrdom, as figurative, is dying daily to the Adamic. As literal, it is laying down our lives sacrificially, an offering toward his righteous final judgment.

It is our calling to increase in thankfulness, forgiveness, and repentance, and, as the Lord allows, greater understanding and perfected worship. All of this is facilitated by the Holy Ghost operation that moves us toward the state of a finished sensitivity of conscience toward God; *"No guile . . . without fault"* (Revelation 14:5). That is maturity. That is Perfection. That is Overcoming.

In closing: Some say we are positionally sinless, or perfect, in the sense that we are covered by the redemptive blood of Christ. The detail of that may be argued; but, in terms of imputed sin, judgment, and wrath, we are not sinners. That "Grace" is confirmed by Scripture. Briefly, *"For the Father judgeth no man, but hath committed all judgment unto the Son"* (John 5:22). The essence being: We have a respite, a stay; time given to overcome and be perfected. All in the name of Jesus and covered by his blood. Let us redeem the time.

CHAPTER 5

Resurrection

To Believe and Embrace: The Defining Step of Faith

GOD'S PLAN AND INTENT toward his creation is that those written in the Book of Life be raised to life with at least the *"earnest"* of citizenship in the New Heaven and the New Earth. Resurrection is the means to that end. Resurrection is altogether integral to God's plan. This is not a presumptuous statement as though we speak on our own. The Word of God declares this truth and he ordains that it be declared to all of humanity.

A resurrection event is God bringing deceased souls into the estate of conscious life. There is no resurrection outside God's register of people known and remembered. Only those written in his book of remembrance will come forth. Again, resurrection is altogether integral to God's plan. Call it an advanced directive in the Message of the Good News. Without resurrection, God's due process could not be *"finished."* The glory of a finished product is made an actuality by the resurrection. *"Concerning his Son Jesus Christ our Lord . . . declared to be the Son of God with power, according to the spirit of holiness,* <u>*by the resurrection from the dead*</u>*"* (Romans 1:4, 5).

This matter of *"finished"* is "pith and marrow" to going on to perfection. The worthy Saints of Matthew 27:52, 53 resurrected and went on to perfection with the ministering of the Early Rain Church. Later, they did die and did go, alive-in-Spirit, to the bosom of the Father. They will reappear at the First Resurrection unto immortality and Celestial habitation.

The King James Version uses the word *resurrection* forty-one times. Thirty-nine times it is translated from the Greek word *anastasis*; meaning "to stand up" and, as literally implied, "to resurrect." Figuratively, it indicates a recovery of some sort. One time, it is translated from the Greek word *egeris*; a resurgence. One time, it is translated from the Greek word *exanastasis*; a rising from death. The KJV Old Testament does not use the word *resurrection*.

It is unlikely that an exhaustive word study would add much helpful knowledge. More likely, a better understanding of the context will give the reader added insight.

In the overview, please understand that this article is not an "easy read." The doctrine of resurrection is primary in God's plan and worthy of our time and study.

Specified Usage of the Word Resurrection

Nowhere in the Old Testament is there an instance of a *from-the-grave resurrection*; that is, a dead person reviving, or reappearing, after having been committed to the grave. A related factor mentioned in Scripture is that the body experience decomposition. Jesus did not *"see corruption"* (Psalms 16:10). However, he was committed to the grave. The dead soldier coming back to life after touching Elisha's bones, as given in 2 Kings 13:21, does not qualify; nor does the appearance of Samuel in 1 Samuel 28:15. Old Testament coming-back to-life events are recorded, but not from death and having been committed to the grave. To wit: Elijah raised the son of the Zarephath widow from death, but not from the grave (1 Kings 17:22). Elisha raised the son of the Shunammite woman from death, but not from the grave (2 Kings 4:32, 35).

New Testament instances are given where the dead were restored to life, but not all were from-the-grave resurrections as we will treat the subject going forward. Jesus, Peter, Paul, and possibly the other apostles raised people from death. Lazarus' resurrection in John 11:43, 44, does qualify as a resurrection from-the-grave. Again, implicit is the idea of "corruption."

The treatment of resurrection as being from-the-grave will serve to simplify and more exactly address our usage of the word. In John 5:28, Jesus used the point *"in the graves"* to distinguish between a literal resurrection and the figurative resurrection of the previous verses.

Lazarus

The resurrection of Lazarus was the first instance of a resurrection from-the-grave. Martha stated, *"Lord, by this time he stinketh"* (John 11:39), which clearly indicates that he was graveyard-dead.

An important fact needs to be stated here: Jesus was the first of the First Fruits, not Lazarus. Jesus' resurrection is distinguished from all others; being that, as first of the First Fruits, he continues alive for evermore. Luke, in Acts 13:34, writes, *"And as concerning that he raised him up from the dead, now no more to return to corruption"* That is a qualifying statement: *"Now no more to return to corruption,"* Lazarus eventually died and returned to dust. Jesus, the first of the First Fruits, did not return to the grave, nor did He *"see corruption"* (Acts 2:27).

An added feature in this discussion: In the parable of the rich man and Lazarus, Luke 16:19–31, the rich man said, *"If one went unto them from the dead, they will repent."*

It seems more than coincidental that a person of the same name did resurrect from the dead, and what was the verdict of the rich-in-tradition Jews? It reads plainly in John 12:10, 11: *"The chief priest consulted that they might put Lazarus also to death; Because that by reason of him many of the Jews went away, and believed on Jesus."* Lazarus was added to the enemy's kill list.

Jesus was the second to resurrect from the grave. He was the second witness fulfilling the judgment requirement and condemned the Jews expressly for their rejection of the resurrection.

Resurrection was the proof and pith and marrow of the life message Jesus preached and demonstrated to the Jews. It is noteworthy that Lazarus' resurrection occupies a special place in Christ's ministry and in God's purpose.

The reality of a resurrection from-the-grave, and an <u>eventual return to the grave, as per Lazarus</u>, leads us to discuss the resurrection of Saints who resurrected after Jesus' resurrection.

The Reappearing of Old Testament Saints

Mathew 27:52, 53—*"And the graves were opened; and many bodies of the saints which slept arose, And came out of the graves after his resurrection, and went into the holy city, and appeared unto many."*

Job 19:26 states, *"And though after my skin worms destroy this body, yet in my flesh shall I see God."* Job held the hope of a resurrection, as did Daniel. *"But go thou thy way till the end be: for thou shalt rest, and stand in thy lot at the end of the days"* (Daniel 12:13).

Isaiah 26:19— *"Thy dead men shall live, together with my dead body shall they arise. Awake and sing, ye that dwell in dust: for thy dew is as the dew of herbs, and the earth shall cast out the dead."*

The context, starting with Isaiah 26:12, reaches forward to God's purpose toward the believing and the unbelieving in the matter of life and death. Verse 20, relates to a return to the safekeeping of the grave for those who rest or sleep in Christ, till judgment is accomplished. That is, *"Come, my people, enter thou into thy chambers, and shut thy doors about thee: hide thyself as it were for a little moment, until the indignation be overpast."* This speaks expressly to the Saints of Matthew 27:52.

Matthew 8:11 states, *"And I say unto you, That many shall come from the east and west, and shall sit down with Abraham, and Isaac, and Jacob, in the kingdom of heaven."* Likewise, Luke 13: 28, 29, *"Ye shall see Abraham, and Isaac, and Jacob, and all the prophets, in the kingdom of God, and you yourselves thrust out. And they shall come from the east, and from the west, and from the north, and from the south, and shall sit down in the kingdom of God."*

1 Corinthians 15:6—The apostle Paul connects back to the time following Jesus' resurrection: *"After that, he was seen of above five hundred brethren at once; of whom the greater part remain unto this present, but some are fallen asleep."* Paul is writing over fifteen years after that resurrection, so, as per Lazarus and as per Isaiah 26:20, some of the resurrected Old Testament Saints, at the time of his writing, had fallen asleep (died).

In 1 Thessalonians 4:13–15, these and others are addressed; the *"dead in Christ."* 13. *"But I would not have you to be ignorant, brethren, concerning them which are asleep, that ye sorrow not, even as others which have no hope. 14. For if we believe that Jesus died and rose again, even so them also which sleep in Jesus will God bring with him. 15. For this we say unto you by the word of the Lord, that we which are alive and remain unto the coming of the Lord shall not prevent them which are asleep."* These deceased being addressed refer to those who are ordained to be partakers of the First Resurrection, reappearing unto immortality and celestial rank.

Hebrews 9:15 states, concerning Christ's mediation, before his advent, *"They which are called might receive the promise of eternal inheritance."* These, the called, would include the resurrected Saints of Matthew 27:52.

In Hebrews 11, Paul writes of these faith-believing Saints of the Old Testament era. Verse 35 states, *"Women received their dead raised to life again: and others were tortured, not accepting deliverance; that they might obtain a better resurrection."* Verses 39–40 state, *"And these all, having obtained a good report through faith, received not the promise: God having provided some better thing for us, that they without us should not be made perfect."* They were ordained of God to obtain that *"better resurrection"* and go on to perfection; because *"they without us should not be made perfect."* The *"us"* were the Early Rain Apostolic Ministry.

Thoughts Relating to the Event

The logistics relating to the resurrection of Matthew 27:52 may seem cumbersome: hundreds of people resurrecting within a short time frame. Would not that have overwhelmed the population of Jerusalem? Unlikely. Consider the cities that presently, on special occasions, double and triple their population with no adverse result. So it was in the Jerusalem area in feast times. Accommodating the stay-over believers and the resurrected saints would not be problematic in light of the temporary communism where they *"had all things common"* (Acts 2:44; 4:32). We understand the need and reason: so that the believers could continue in Jerusalem to glean the fundamentals of the new message. These, gaining the new Gospel Message and returning home to publish the Gospel, later provided the apostle Paul the needed doors to begin evangelizing the Gentiles. We can reasonably include some of the converted returnees of seventeen nations (Acts 2:9–11). The point being: Adding hundreds to the Jerusalem population would not be overwhelming, nor would the people's necessities go wanting.

Some of the resurrected saints eventually return to their native soil, be it near or distant. If the Saints arose in the proximity of their burial, then, them coming *"from the east, and from the west, and from the north, and from the south,"* would have included a travel-time consideration. In Exodus 13:19, Joseph had given instruction, *"God will surely visit you; and ye shall carry up my bones away hence with you."* That request was granted. He was later buried in Shechem, a closer proximity to Jerusalem (Joshua 24:32). Travel, postresurrection, may have been a consideration regarding his place of burial.

What about the confusion factor? Would not the tradition-minded Jews have divided out and set forward a worship toward Abraham, or Moses, or the Prophets and other Old Testament greats? Would not the Apostles have been overshadowed and or cast aside? Answer: No. God would not be so unfair to the Church and those resurrected to give them immediate and complete recall.

The most meaningful aspect of this potential to hive off is the fact that those notables of the Old Testament were not covetous of leadership or exaltation. They were humble men, broken in heart and humble of spirit. They did not entertain "position," nor would they have argued with Jesus' statement, *"Verily I say unto you, Among them that are born of women there hath not risen a greater than John the Baptist: notwithstanding <u>he that is least in the kingdom of heaven is greater than he</u>"* (Matthew 11:11). On that point: When Jesus appeared to these saints in 1 Corinthians 15:6, he likely explained that they resurrected as servants under the law. Their lot was to join company and integrate with the Church and be *"born-again"* as New Covenant Sons of God. That was not demeaning, just right order.

What about the identity factor? You might argue, if they did not know who they were, then, would not their reappearance be meaningless? Again, not so; consider how many memories of your formative years are lost. Yet you are very much yourself. Consider people that lose memory by virtue of amnesia or other causes. They are not necessarily altered in terms of disposition or character. This approach is not cold, impersonal or unreal. In due time, with the maturity of the situation and the individuals, a full, or nearly full, recollection would be forthcoming. Such recall, immediate or delayed, would be prescribed by God and done with total benefit to the Church and the individual. A predestinated going-on-to-perfection purpose would remain un-altered and effectual. Again, our God is not cold, impersonal, or Orwellian. While it is not the present item of interest, this point of understanding could be elaborated upon, and even yield added detail toward explaining the general nature of the resurrection event.

The foundational thought is that those under the Law who were deemed worthy, by faith and God's favor, to be part of the very elect first fruits and first resurrection were raised here so that they could be partakers of the Early Rain Ministry and attain overcomer status. Was *"above five hundred brethren at once"* (1 Corinthians 15:6), a close approximation or was the number much greater? I do not know. It is only reasonable that those few hundred Saints of Matthew 27:52 would be only a fraction of the total Old Testament Saints that were heirs to a resurrection. Many thousands will come forth in the day of the resurrection and in the final resurrection; or, as per Revelation 20:5, *"the rest of the dead."* Again, these relatively few of the Matthew 27:52 group, were the chosen of God for their graduating to the "first resurrection" status, eventually being the *"man child"* (Revelation 12:5) and *"bride, the Lamb's wife"* (Revelation 21:9).

A principal understanding involving this particular resurrection event is that these eventual overcomers, in time, died and were buried, but with full assurance of the blessed first resurrection reward. Suffice to say, the resurrection of Matthew 27:52 is embraced as biblically set forth. It is a God-select number of Old Testament Saints who were candidates to the high calling.

Beyond this singular event, pertaining to the worthies of the Old Testament, is the portrayal of the ongoing resurrection scenario that will be typical in the millennium period. To wit: <u>Having an understanding of the resurrection of Matthew 27:52, we are given the portrayal, or basis, for Christ's millennium reign which is a thousand-year resurrection period</u>. People due a resurrection, and a "going-on-to-perfection" reward, will reappear, and, depending on their life-span and timing of their resurrection, will live to the "change" or die but reappear changed in the final resurrection, as blessed unto a new heaven and earth, as terrestrials with eternal life.

This takes us to a discussion of the high calling or bride message, and the select catching away. Beyond the following section, this issue will be revisited later in chapter VIII, 'Troubling Issues.'

CHAPTER 6

The High Calling: Bride Message

The High Watermark Understanding Which Completes the Doctrine

GOD'S PLAN INCLUDES THE *"glory of the celestial"* held in store for his select chosen. This section amplifies on the "bride" or "man child," numbering 144,000. As per Revelation 12:5, *"man child . . . caught up unto God, and to his throne."* One thousand years later, the same 144,000 return as the *"bride"* (Revelation 21:9). They will be the officiation of the New Jerusalem. This section also gives considerable thought to the question of our humanly striving for a graduation to the High Calling, or Bride status. That graduation is from mortal–terrestrial to immortal–celestial, and from having eternal life to immortality status. The overriding consideration brought forth is that the choosing is per God's determination.

The "graduation plan" is hidden truth, and it is the high-water mark relating to resurrection. It is no comfort to the author to know that those rejecting this precept are agreeing to a continuing blind spot in their theology.

This writing gives detail to what I have termed the "high-water mark" of the resurrection subject. That is, the high-calling Bride message and the question of "election or other." Understanding and believing this precious truth is akin to embracing the heartbeat of the whole-of-the-matter pertaining to heaven's plan: God's desire, will, and intent.

The Spirit of the Saint's Endeavors

Concerning our desire for the "high calling," when the truth of the "Bride message" is heard and understood, a person's desire for this calling comes alive in his heart. That message is a revelation of the mystery; a spiritual understanding relating to the Resurrection of the Dead. It is the understanding which reveals, beyond everlasting life and a perfect terrestrial body, that there is a spiritual "Very Elect" that gain immortality and a celestial habitation.

Depending how this truth is presented, a person may conclude that being one of those 144,000 of Revelation 14:1 is the one and only goal worth reaching for, even embracing it with a despising toward anything less. Going forward, that kind of ambition, being a pride-driven mindset, would misdirect and spoil the hope of God's perfect will and plan for our individual lives. The overriding requirement is that the Spirit of Christ, flavored with humility and thankfulness, prevails; without which the endeavor fails. The Spirit-of-the-vision is vital. To wit:

There is a need to understand how the word *strive* is used. We need to know the definition of the word. Strong's Concordance gives us several scriptural references. The English word *strive* is translated from several Greek words. Three examples follow: (1) 1 Timothy 2:5, *athleo* (athlete), to contend, as in competitive games, strive; (2) Luke 13:24, *agonizomai* (agonize), to struggle, as for a prize, labor fervently, strive; and, (3) 2 Timothy 2:24, *machomai* (macho), to quarrel, dispute, fight, strive.

Scripture portrays no contest or pitting of saint against saint. Indeed; Romans 15:30 states; *"strive together."* That is, agonize together.

For certain, we need to know <u>how</u> the word *strive* is defined or used before applying it to the idea of "striving" for the bride.' We must press or strive to overcome this world and the lust thereof, but in the sense of agonize and discipline and not in the sense of macho (fight); and, then, having run <u>lawfully</u>, we understand that the prize is <u>of God</u>. The "of God" brings us to the second point.

When we say *strive for the bride*, it may be implied that <u>we</u> strive and accomplish the goal. We must keep in mind that <u>God</u> is in charge of who attains to the bride of Christ. What we term *Bride*, is the very elect, the high calling, and it is <u>God</u> that gives a special measure of Grace to whomever he wants to, and however much he wants to give; that is the accomplishing of the matter. Correct thinking is that all overcoming and attaining to the goal will be in terms of <u>his</u> added measure of grace and mercy. Primary and foremost: <u>God Is Sovereign</u>! This "right understanding" keeps us humble and balanced. When using the term *strive*, we are not to think that <u>our</u> striving is the main or only criteria. <u>It is an election</u>; <u>God's choice</u>. Agreed, we must strive, press, and reach out for perfection, life, and Christ-likeness; all the while, understand that such effort, in itself, is not the sole requirement and basis for attaining to the Very Elect, Bride, and High Calling. Rest assured, it is required that we "run" the race and "will" to be obedient. However, to preach striving-for-the-Bride as a matter of self-determination, and that willfully accomplished, is error. Some people read Romans 9:16 as not <u>to</u> him that "willeth," nor <u>to</u> him that "runneth." We need to give pause here and reread the verse. The reward certainly is to him that runs and wills. The Scripture says expressly, *"It is not <u>of</u> him that willeth, nor <u>of</u> him that runneth"* This Scripture actually depicts a person running and determining to reach the mark. Nonetheless, our confession is *"but <u>of God that sheweth mercy</u>."* The power and glory belong to our God and Savior. (It is duly noted that this Scripture is in the context of God's predestined will, but the principle, as stated, is correctly applied.)

The First Resurrection: People and Purpose

The *"very elect"* (Matthew 24:24), or *"bride"* (Revelation 21:9), or *"man child"* (Revelation 12:5), make up the *"firstfruits"* of which Jesus is the first. They comprise, exclusively, the first resurrection. They are the 144,000 of Revelation 14:1. They are *"a great multitude, which no man could number, of all nations, and kindreds, and people, and* tongues, *stood before the throne, and before the Lamb, clothed with white robes, and palms in their hands"* (Revelation 7:9). They *"lived and reigned with Christ a thousand years . . . This is the first resurrection"* (Revelation 20:4, 5). This group is of celestial rank and glory. In 1 Corinthians 15:40, it declares; *"There are also celestial bodies, and bodies terrestrial: but the glory of the celestial is one, and the glory of the terrestrial is another."*

We embrace this select 144,000 as *"a man child, who was to rule all nations with a rod of iron: and her child was caught up unto God, and to his throne"* (Revelation 12:5). We attribute this and like Scriptures to the first resurrection; those being the ones raised to a celestial estate. This understanding of the 144,000 and *"rightly dividing the word of truth"* (2 Timothy 2:15), gives reasonableness and continuity to the resurrection doctrine, discussion, and explanation. Without this understanding, we entertain bizarre portrayals of babies disappearing, pilots missing from the cockpit, cars and trucks wrecking because of persons taken. That kind of thing is not to be entertained, or expected, or thought common to the event of the first resurrection. Repeating, this is a "troubling" issue. It will be revisited in chapter VIII.

The first resurrection, or catching away, pertains to a select 144,000 Saints. It is a literal, exact number because it is the governmental, ruling elect. They are chosen by God, as the Bride of Christ, from the many thousands of overcomers. They are comprised of the hundreds of Old Testament Saints that resurrected with Christ and the additional tens of thousands of the Early Church plus the tens of thousands of the Latter Church.

As to the Bride or Chosen Elect numbered during the *Dark Ages*—that is, the centuries following the Early Rain up to the Latter Rain— we rest in the knowledge that God knows those that are chosen in him, and we trust that those chosen have been perfected by special Holy Ghost direction and power. If otherwise, and if a fivefold ministry is required, then it is certainly God's prerogative to bring them forth in a spiritually fitting future time. Such should be our confession. Those Saints whose lives connect the Early Rain with the Latter Rain are referred to as the "silver thread." It is a similitude not easily understood.

Pertaining to the 144,000, many use the number 42,360 of Ezra 2:64 and Nehemiah 7:66 as a similitude to indicate the Latter Church number. That would indicate the number of the Early Rain Church to be 101,640 (144,000 - 42,360). Such numerical exactness derived from a similitude is not generally embraced. A more likely breakdown of Early–Latter would be two-thirds Early and one-thirds Latter, with no requirement as to being exact.

Following is a quick review as to the makeup and purpose of the first resurrection:

The 144,000 comprise the total of the first resurrection, being made up of hundreds of Old Testament Saints with the tens of thousands of Early Rain Saints, plus the tens of thousands of the Latter Rain Saints with God's choice of those between the Early and Latter Rain: chosen by God from the host of overcomers.

While this number is a small fraction of the multiplied millions that will make heaven their home, yet, it is the high-water "marker" for the resurrection doctrine.

These are ordained to be the second witness, with Christ in his martyrdom, who will judge this world and the angels. In 1 Corinthians 6:2, 3, it states: *"Do ye not know that the saints shall judge the world? . . . Know ye not that we shall judge angels?"* Favored of God and elect of God, *"*the man child*"* of Revelation 12:5, *"they lived and reigned with Christ a thousand years"* (Revelation 20:4).

After one thousand years, in the time frame of *"the restitution of all things, which God hath spoken by the mouth of all his holy prophets since the world began"* (Acts 3:21), they are thereafter portrayed as *"*the bride, *the Lamb's wife"* (Revelation 21:9).

The First Resurrection Event: Time and Setting

1 Corinthians 15 has been termed "the resurrection chapter." The "first resurrection" is the subject of this chapter. In 15:52, it states, *"In a moment, in the twinkling of an eye, at the last trump: for the trumpet shall sound, and the dead shall be raised incorruptible, and we shall be changed."*

Paul restates the same, with added insights.

1 Thessalonians 4:15–17—15. *"For this we say unto you by the word of the Lord, that we which are alive and remain unto the coming of the Lord shall not prevent them which are asleep. 16. For the Lord himself shall descend from heaven with a shout, with the voice of the archangel, and with the trump of God: and the dead in Christ shall rise first: 17. Then we which are alive and remain shall be caught up together with them in the clouds, to meet the Lord in the air: and so shall we ever be with the Lord."*

If we combine the facts of these two scriptural references, we can validate the fact that these Scriptures refer to "the first resurrection." They are changed from *"mortal"* to *"immortality"* (1 Corinthians 15:54). This is a resurrection to celestial, immortal status, whereas the final resurrection pertains to mortals attaining eternal life. Furthermore, given correct context, we see that 1 Corinthians 15:48, 49, distinguishes between the *"earthy"* and the *"heavenly."* Expressly; *"as we have borne the image of the earthly, we shall also bear the image of the heavenly."* "Earthy" is referring to the terrestrial, mortals, and "heavenly" is referring to the celestial, immortals. These two passages give an as-per-the-Scripture understanding of the event.

The *"last trump"* (1 Corinthians 15:52), and *"the trump of God"* (1 Thessalonians 4:16), are one and the same. The last trump, sixth, is the end of Gentile times and sounds in the time frame immediately preceding the final or seventh trumpet. The final, seventh trumpet is the initial sounding of the millennial reign of Christ. Six is man's number and the last trumpet concludes the 6,000 years of man's reign. On that point: It is noteworthy that the sixth and seventh trumpets follow in fast succession. To wit: *"The second woe (sixth trumpet) is past; and, behold, the third woe (seventh trumpet) cometh quickly"* (Revelation 11:14).

Revelation 11: The Timeline of the First Resurrection

3 ½ yrs. Latter Rain: begins when ten kings	3 ½ yrs. Martyrdom	Rapture	7 ½ yrs. God's wrath
receive power & Gentiles occupy Jerusalem	of the Saints of God		7 thunders & 7 vials

Verse 1—*"And there was given me a reed like unto a rod: and the angel stood, saying, Rise, and measure the temple of God, and the altar, and them that worship therein."* This declares that the Jewish people and traditional worship fall within God's measure. And, regarding any Gentile imposition, the Jew's leadership would be agreeable only if there was a hands-off policy concerning people and worship.

(The mention of temple and altar indicates a future third temple. Beyond that, there is the possibility three future building sites will be allotted on a reconfigured holy mount: Jewish, Christian, and the present Moslem mosque. Reasonably, the Papacy would claim front and center of the Christian site. All things considered; not God's perfect will, but allowed for the purpose of fulfilling all judgment. These are possibilities, and such matters fall into the category of conjecture.)

Verse 2—*"But the court which is without the temple leave out, and measure it not; for it is given unto the Gentiles: and the holy city shall they tread under foot forty and two months."* Months are "moon"-related and, thus, refer to the Jews–Law. Forty-two months is three-and-a-half years. The court relates to the natural geography: Occupation by the Gentile powers will be a volatile condition that God will allow. It is an unknown as to what will precipitate an international demand for such an action: likely a serious and threatening breach of world order on the part of some Middle Eastern nation. An occupation of Jerusalem would mark the beginning of the last hour. This reference is to the occupying force that will supposedly guarantee peace. In 1 Thessalonians 5:3, it states, *"For when they shall say, Peace and safety; then sudden destruction cometh upon them, as travail upon a woman with child; and they shall not escape."* The context is the time of *"the day of the Lord so cometh as a thief in the night"* (1 Thessalonians 5:2).

Verse 3—*"And I will give power unto my two witnesses, and they shall prophesy a thousand two hundred and threescore days, clothed in sackcloth."* 1,260 days is three-and-a-half years as per 360 days/year. Days are "sun"-related and, thus, refers to the Church–Grace. The three-and-a-half years of verse 2 and verse 3 are coincidental not consecutive. In this time frame of three-and-one-half years the nation of Israel will, for a season, lose sovereign control of their land. Simultaneously, the Latter Church will come totally under the sovereign reign of Christ, ministering the concluding judgment to the Gentile world. To wit: The sun is going down on the Gentiles as they are judged, while the sun is coming up on the Jews as they are judged. This three-and-a-half years is the time referred to in Isaiah 21:12, *"The watchman said, The morning cometh, and also the night:"* This three-and-a-half years is the beginning of the last hour. It is that same time that begins the *"one hour"* of Revelation 17:12, when *"the ten kings . . . receive power as kings one hour with the beast."* The two events are concurrent. This initial three-and-a-half years is the time of the Latter Rain, and the occupation of Jerusalem; also, being the Mideast time of *"Peace and safety."* Again, 1 Thessalonians 5:3.

Verse 4—*"These are the two olive trees, and the two candlesticks standing before the God of the earth."* Verses 4 thru 12 portray two individuals. *"Two prophets"* versus ten, or, as per similitude; Michael and Gabriel, or Moses and Christ, or the Old and New Testaments, or the Church which would imbibe all of these named. The detail of this touches the "Throne of God" discussion which approaches what I term the "ineffability factor." We can state the obvious: Michael was Archaeon, or primary Angel, as a sort of fiduciary of the Old Testament, both "Conscience" and "Law." Gabriel ministered toward the New Testament dispensation of Grace. Repeating; Moses was *"mediator"* of the law. *"It* (the Law) *was ordained by angels in the hand of a mediator* (Moses)*"* (Galatians 3:19). And, as is Christ, *"He is the mediator of the new testament"* (Hebrews 9:15). The Latter Rain Ministry, of three-and-a-half years duration, reflects all of the above; all *"that stand in the presence of God."* The beginning of the latter rain is the initiation of the fulfilling of all types and similitudes. All of heaven and earth will be on station for this Latter Rain Church's concluding message.

Verses 5 and 6 declare the power of God to finish the message and the judgment. Verses 7–10 speak of an accomplished mission, *"testimony,"* allowing a time of martyrdom for about three-and-a-half years. This is the time of the seventh beast having thus transitioned to the eighth beast, as per gaining the ungodly addition of demonic possession and power. This is a time of martyrdom of Saints; the time of *"should be killed as they were, should be fulfilled"* (Revelation 6:11).

Verses 11, 12, 13, and 14 give the end of the three-and-a-half years of martyrdom and the event of the resurrection and reappearing of the very elect; also, their ascension *"up to heaven."* The earthquake that follows declares a *"glory to the God of heaven."* Then, *"The second woe is past; and, behold, the third woe cometh quickly."*

Repeating: Revelation 12:5 refers to the Church and the Very Elect, *"And she brought forth a man child, who was to rule all nations with a rod of iron: and her child was caught up unto God, and to his throne."* See Revelation 20:6, *"Blessed and holy is he that hath part in the first resurrection: on such the second death hath no power, but they shall be priests of God and of Christ, and shall reign with him a thousand years."* Also, in 1 Corinthians 15:52, 53: *"And the dead shall be raised incorruptible, and we shall be changed. For this corruptible must put on incorruption, and this mortal must put on immortality."*

Thus, the event of the first resurrection takes place at the sixth, or "last trumpet," being the end of Gentile times. That sounding approximates the initiation of the seventh trumpet, being the beginning of the millennial reign of Christ. It is the beginning of, as per similitude, the seven-and-a-half-year Davidic reign in Hebron, and that seventh is a dispensing of seven thunders and seven vials until Armageddon. The first resurrection is very select and involves 144,000 souls. It is an explicit number. It is the number pertaining to "government." They are changed, at the event, from terrestrial to celestial, from mortal to immortal.

The Final Resurrection: Who Will Resurrect?

The "final resurrection" includes untold millions of souls resurrecting. They *resurrect*, or appear before the Judgment Seat, being terrestrials. They are judged unto either eternal life, or eternal death. It will include all the souls registered in God's "remembrance," especially including Old Testament era believers, and the New Testament era believers; all being heirs to a resurrection, but who were not partakers of the first resurrection.

This is a brief introductory statement, and further detail is given in the following section.

Revelation 20: The Timeline, Events of the Final Resurrection

The 7th day millennium has ended and the 8th day begins with Satan loosed for <u>3½ yrs.</u> to gather the opposition against God.

After which, the devil is judged. ~3½ yrs. later; final resurrection

Revelation 20:7–10 gives the postmillennial event of Satan being loosed and the deception that leads to the gathering to battle of Gog and Magog. In the end, it is a no-battle judgment of the nations' population of evil people, and Satan.

7. *"And When the thousand years are expired, Satan shall be loosed out of his prison. 8. And shall go out to deceive the nations which are in the four quarters of the earth, Gog and Magog, to gather them together to battle: the number of whom is as the sand of the sea. 9. And they went up on the breadth of the earth, and compassed the camp of the saints about, and the beloved city: and fire came down from God out of heaven, and devoured them. 10. And the devil that deceived them was cast into the lake of fire and brimstone, where the beast and the false prophet are, and shall be tormented day and night for ever and ever."*

Regarding the time of the beginning of the eighth day: It begins with a period termed *"a little season"* (Revelation 20:3). *"He should deceive the nations no more, till the thousand years should be fulfilled: and after that he must be loosed* <u>a little season</u>.*" A little season* is taken to be three-and-a-half years. In order to substantiate the "little season" as being three-and-a-half years, we go to Revelation 6:9–11. *"And when he had opened the fifth seal, I saw under the altar the souls of them that were slain for the word of God, and for the testimony which they held: And they cried with a loud voice, saying, How long, O Lord, holy and true, dost thou not judge and avenge our blood on them that dwell on the earth? And white robes were given unto every one of them; and it was said unto them, that they should rest yet for* <u>a little season,</u> *until their fellow servants also and their brethren that should be killed as they were, should be fulfilled."* That period of martyrdom is three-and-a-half years. Thus, we use the term "little season" of Revelation 20:3 to mean three-and-a-half years.

Revelation 20:11–15—The final resurrection/judgment is depicted in these verses. 11. *"And I saw a great white throne, and him that sat on it, from whose face the earth and the heaven fled away; and there was found no place for them. 12. And I saw the dead, small and great, stand before God; and the books were opened: and another book was opened, which is the book of life: and the dead were judged out of those things which were written in the books, according to their works. 13. And the sea gave up the dead which were in it; and death and hell delivered up the dead which were in them: and they were judged every man according to their works. 14. And death and hell were cast into the lake of fire. This is the* second death. *15. And whosoever was not found written in the book of life was cast into the lake of fire."*

It is necessary, for the sake of understanding the final judgment, to know the meaning of *"second death"* mentioned above, in verse 14. Ephesians 2:1 states, *"who were 'dead in trespasses and sin.'"* There is no "final" resurrection in that estate of being "dead to God." Those persons are not in the book of life. Then, if by conversion, or resurrection, they are made "alive to God," they are, thus, children of the resurrection. Now, we can say they "were dead" and are now "alive." Then, if a person, of his own volition takes himself out of the estate of being "in Christ," and "falls away," to the extent they frustrate God's grace, then, their name is subject to being blotted out of the book of life. In such case, they are rendered "dead," having no resurrection. That is, dead a second time, or *"twice dead,"* as per Jude 12. That is another way of saying *"second death."* This is not to say the grace of God is humanly flaunted, nor are we without full assurance. Again, a person who is unconverted and faithless is in the state of second death from his beginning. Restated: A person, having never known God, does not have his name in the book of life and is in the condition of second death, due no resurrection, rather only final and eternal death. Relating to the treatment of the "hell" subject: These statements approach "annihilation doctrine," and that is a "hot spot" and that is "troubling." It is discussed later in chapter VIII.

Verse 12 denotes the blessed who are judged unto eternal life. *"And I saw* the dead, small and great, *stand before God; and the books were opened: and another book was opened, which is the book of life: and* the dead *were judged out of those things which were written in the books, according to their works."* At this point we are three-and-a-half to seven-and-a-half years into the eighth day.

At this point it is needful to go back one thousand years to the beginning of the seventh-day millennium reign of Christ. Specifically, we need to go back to the first seven-and-a-half years into the seventh day. The reason being: We need to connect the beginning seven-and-a-half years of the seventh day with the beginning seven-and-a-half years of the eighth day. Scripture treats the time frame as one day, and there is continuity of purpose in that one-thousand-year day. It is the day of the Lord. It is the day of "resurrection" and the time of the final resurrection and judgment. For the moment, we are back to the time of the last trumpet of Gentile time and the catching away, first resurrection, which followed quickly on the end of the fifth seal time frame of three-and-a-half years mentioned earlier pertaining to Revelation 6:9–11. The last trumpet of Gentile time includes a quick but terrible and consequential war, prefaced by the catching away. Events move quickly to the seventh trumpet or third woe, which is the beginning of the millennium; the time frame of Revelation 11:18; seven-and-a-half years. This seven-and-a-half years is a time of the wrath of God and that is the time of the seven thunders and the seven vials. It is also the time of the Bride and the marriage supper of the Lamb. The first events of the final resurrection era would have to begin at the ending of that seven-and-a-half-year time frame. The seven-and-a-half years belong to the Lord and his Bride. To wit: Revelation 11:18

is a connected Scripture which states, *"And the nations were angry, and thy wrath is come, and the time of* <u>the dead</u>, *that they should be judged and that thou shouldest give reward unto thy servants the prophets, and to the saints, and them that fear thy name,* <u>small and great.</u>*"* This is the time of the third woe, and seventh angel. It is the starting of the seventh day, millennial reign of Christ. It is a period of seven-and-a-half years. It is the Hebron-time when King David reigned, before he took Jerusalem. *"David was thirty years old when he began to reign, and he reigned forty years. In Hebron he reigned over Judah seven years and six months: and in Jerusalem he reigned thirty and three years over all Israel and Judah"* (2 Samuel 5:4, 5). That seven-and-a-half years was part of his forty-year reign. Likewise, it is a part of the millennium reign of Christ. It is a similitude, indicating Christ will take Jerusalem, in the events of Armageddon, seven-and-a-half years into the millennium. Again, these seven-and-a-half years is the Bride time, the marriage supper of the Lamb. It was given as a type in Genesis 24:67, when Isaac takes Rebekah into his mother's tent, in Hebron. This passage, Revelation 11:18, speaks of giving reward to *"thy servants, the prophets, and to the saints, and them that fear thy name."* These are the blessed heirs of a good resurrection. The similar wording of Revelation 20:12 lends credence to these, *"the dead, small and great,"* likewise being the blessed-unto-eternal life. This time frame of seven-and-a-half years does cover the celestial half-hour and those blessed and chosen, but we are concentrating here on the terrestrial aspect; that is, the final resurrection era, initiated at the end of this seven-and-a-half years. As per the point being expressed; Revelation 11:18 connects the start of the millennial reign of Christ with the eighth-day final resurrection and judgment.

Note: If three-and-a-half years is a little season, then seven-and-a-half years may be the conclusion of the season of all things. Thus, the time of the final resurrection/judgment, being in the eighth day, may be within the first seven-and-a-half years.

Repeating, Revelation 11:18, *"the time of the dead, that they should be judged"* is at the end of the up-front seven-and-a-half years of the seventh day. The final resurrection/judgment of Revelation 20:7–15, is about a thousand years later in the beginning seven-and-a-half years of the eighth day.

Repeating for emphasis: We are looking at a *"time of the dead . . . small and great,"* a resurrection and judgment depicted at the first of the seventh day, with similar words spoken regarding the early on eighth day final resurrection/judgment. That is a thousand-year period of time.

Note: The seventh-day millennium is a thousand-year "time" of resurrection. Without stretching the definition, *"time,"* being *karios* in Greek, could be a time frame or season. It is the <u>day of the Lord;</u> a thousand-year day. And our Lord is the <u>resurrection and the life</u>. That is not a play on words. It is <u>what he does</u> and <u>who he is</u>. That thousand-year day begins with the events of Revelation 11:18 and ends in the time frame of the final resurrection/judgment of Revelation 20:7–15.

The conclusion of this scriptural discussion is: There will likely be a resurrection, terrestrial, seven-and-a-half years into the beginning of the seventh day and continue into the millennium. It would necessarily follow the time of the first resurrection, celestial, by about seven-and-a-half years. If and how extensive that early on terrestrial resurrection would be, we do not know. It is God's choosing. In total, the final resurrection could include many millions. That is also a figure we do not know.

Considering the thousand-year day of the Lord's reign, mankind's health and longevity of life will increase as the seventh day progresses. Scripture indicates that in the thousand-year "day of the Lord," people will overcome and eventually die; but in a blessed estate. Others will fail to gain victory, and as the prophet said, *"The sinner being a hundred years old shall be accursed"* (Isaiah 65:20).

Consider, as the millennium progresses, the atmosphere will increase with millions of tons of water vapor, somewhat depleting the seas. The result will be increased protection from the sun's radiation and increased atmospheric pressure, possibly fivefold, which would dramatically increase the oxygen content in the blood. That would be an increased health benefit for all. The millions of tons of water released back into the atmosphere would dramatically increase the land-to-seas ratio. Similarly, collapsed and depleted underground aquifers will be restored and replenished. We will likely see a return to 360-day years and thirty-day lunar cycles.

I am not a scientist, nor do I feel able or led to go beyond the simple science relating to this return to the pre-Flood, pre-sin state of the earth and man. We know it will happen. The earth and mankind will be restored to the state God originally intended.

As mankind's spirit grows in his connection with God, his dominion will increase from command over his carnal nature to include dominion over nature itself. Thus, we will see the fulfillment: *"The wolf and the lamb shall feed together and the lion shall eat straw like the bullock"* (Isaiah 65:25). Also, *"And the sucking child shall play on the hole of the asp, and the weaned child shall put his hand on the cockatrice' den"* (Isaiah 11:8).

This spiritual progression will be experienced only in the realm of the earth that is submitted to our Lord and Savior. If a person is resurrected outside that realm, they should endeavor with all their strength to get themselves and any associations moved to that blessed geography.

Let us humbly confess: The resurrection *"time"* and the earth's restoration are not meant to accommodate man and beast so much as it is to facilitate God's plan of the ages. *"Thou art worthy, O Lord, to receive glory and honour and power: for thou hast created all things, and for thy pleasure they are and were created"* (Revelation 4:11).

The concept set forth by the resurrection of Matthew 27:52 gives the necessary guidelines; primarily demonstrating that overcomers do die and, being heirs to the resurrection, come forth later. That scenario applies to the millennium day of the Lord, from start to finish.

This being said, we continue the final resurrection/judgment subject, as per Revelation 20, going forward to the end of the seventh and into the eighth-day time frame.

Repeating Revelation 20:11–15: 11: *"And I saw a great white throne, and him that sat on it, from whose face the earth and the heaven fled away; and there was found no place for them. 12. And I saw the dead, small and great, stand before God; and the books were opened: and another book was opened, which is the book of life: and the dead were judged out of those things which were written in the books, according to their works. 13. And the sea gave up the dead which were in it;*

and death and hell delivered up the dead which were in them: and they were judged every man according to their works. 14. And death and hell were cast into the lake of fire. This is the second death. 15. And whosoever was not found written in the book of life was cast into the lake of fire."

Verse 12 denotes those judged unto eternal life. *"And I saw* the dead, small and great, *stand before God; and the books were opened: and another book was opened, which is the book of life: and the dead were judged out of those things which were written in the books, according to their works."* This pertains to those who are "the dead in Christ" status. It is understood that this term used in 1 Thessalonians 4:16 pertains explicitly to the first resurrection, but the principle and status is: Heirs to a blessed resurrection, be it celestial or terrestrial.

Verses 13–15 conclude the judgment unto eternal damnation. *"And the sea gave up the dead which were in it; and death and hell delivered up the dead which were in them: and they were judged every man according to their works. And death and hell were cast into the lake of fire. This is the second death. And whosoever was not found written in the book of life was cast into the lake of fire."*

This Scripture, per context, puts the final judgment after the gathering-to-battle of Gog and Magog. It is after *"the devil that deceived them was cast into the lake of fire and brimstone, where the beast and the false prophet are"* (Revelation 20:10).

Thus, the final resurrection/judgment is in the first season of the eighth day. That is the first years of the eighth thousand years. At the time of the final resurrection there will be multitudes of living overcomers. Comparable to the *"alive and remain"* of 1 Thessalonians 4:15, these are alive and well on the earth. Remember, the evil and defiled are annihilated, and the devil is judged as stated in Revelation 20:9, 10: *"And they went up on the breadth of the earth, and compassed the camp of the saints about, and the beloved city: and fire came down from God out of heaven, and* devoured them. *And the devil that deceived them was* cast into the lake of fire and brimstone, *where the beast and the false prophet are, and shall be tormented day and night for ever and ever."*

These multitudes of living overcomers will, at the time of the final resurrection, gain eternal life as terrestrials, just as the living very elect gained immortality at the time of the first resurrection. See 1 Corinthians 15:51: *"We shall not all sleep, but we shall all be changed."*

Those resurrected from death, being in Christ and blessed, will enter into the *"new heaven and a new earth"* (Revelation 21:1). They will acclimate to eternal life and the heaven-on-earth estate, as terrestrials; married to the earth, as God would have it.

Note: Concerning the resurrection/judgment of the condemned of verses 13–15: In verse 12, we see the resurrected as standing. In verses 13–15, those are not standing and possibly not present in person. They may well be brought forth to consciousness to experience their fate, but it is also possible that they will be brought forth as a class or classification of people who do not literally stand or gain consciousness, but are nevertheless judged. However that is accomplished, settle it in your minds: It is God's determination and it is a final judgment.

An additional thought that relates to the plan of God and our vision: Revelation 21:9–27 reveals the *"bride, the Lamb's wife . . . that great city, the holy Jerusalem, descending out of heaven from God."* This is the portrayal of the bride, celestial, coming to earth at the time of the *"restitution of all things"* (Acts 3:21). It is God's plan of the ages. Presently it is *"Jerusalem which is above is free, which is the mother of us all"* (Galatians 4:26). The Church is portrayed as the wife of Christ, and our mother, as sons of God, because we embrace the heavenly vision *"which is above."* This is the heart of our bride message. They are very elect: the chosen of God, married to Christ.

The final resurrection/judgment and all that pertains to it, including the restoration of the Jew, is also a bride message. It is the plan of God that reinstates the people, terrestrial, as married to the land. *"Thou shalt be called Hephzibah, and thy land Beulah: for the Lord delighted in thee, and thy land shall be married. For as a young man marrieth a virgin, so shall thy sons marry thee: and as the bridegroom rejoiceth over the bride, so shall thy God rejoice over thee"* (Isaiah 62:4, 5). It is an earth event whereas the bride-of-Christ message is a soon coming heavenly, celestial event.

The bride message, celestial, relates to the first resurrection. The bride message, terrestrial, relates to the final resurrection/judgment.

In the finality of all things, as per the bride messages, plural, they are the property of one God and his Son Jesus Christ. Their continuance is a "unity" for God's glory and pleasure and the Resurrection is a fitting and perfect conclusion to his "Will" and "Plan." God's "Plan," of which we are included, according to His great Grace.

Revelation 7: Giving Added Details Pertaining to Persons, Purpose, and Time of the First and Final Resurrection Events

The following treatment of Revelation 7 aims to add insight to the revelation of the "finishing" of God's plan. While it is repetitive, it is not meant to argue the point of a select rapture. Moving forward in the narrative, we will reference the first and a second, or final, resurrection. The first resurrection might be thought of as a "select rapture." That view is scriptural and doctrinally correct. Without that knowledge, the resurrection event, as portrayed, is chaotic and bizarre. Those who entertain this truth of resurrection doctrine are a minority; typically rejected, even despised. For that reason, it may be set aside by you the reader. There will be no offence in "putting it on the shelf." Please know that there is no offence intended on the part of the writer. Traditional teachings on resurrection are not demeaned or cast down.

This writing does give attention to the timeline within the Book of Revelation. It does not give answers relating to end-time dates AD.

Revelation 7:4–8

The first group of 144,000 from the twelve tribes is exclusively terrestrial Jews. They are sealed unto Christ and comprise the lead government of Israel at Jerusalem. Again, they are fully committed, prepared and "sealed," in Christ. They will initiate the terrestrial vanguard leadership heading into the thousand-year Lord's Day. Almost certainly, they are products of their current generation and these 144,000 include no resurrected individuals. The text indicates that this group of terrestrials have not gained the estate of *"Dieth no more; death hath no dominion over him"* in Romans 6:9. To wit: Scripture indicates they do not have eternal life. As such, they would be replaced, as per a normal lifespan, as the seventh thousand-year day progresses. Howbeit, God is sovereign and that is his to determine. If so be that it is God's will, he can grant these 144,000 terrestrial Jews eternal life at that time, and they could rule on earth throughout the millennium.

Revelation 7:9–17

The second group are the ascended *"man child"* or the *"caught up"* ones in Revelation 12:5. They are the 144,000 of Revelation 14:1. These are the first Resurrection Saints, Elect of God. (They appear, after the seventh one thousand years, as *"descending out of heaven from God"* (Revelation 21:10). They are called *"the bride, the Lamb's wife"* in verse 9.)

The first resurrection is from mortal to immortal and from terrestrial to celestial. It is limited to the 144,000 chosen of God. (For starters, we can reference 1 Corinthians 15:40; then forward with other Scripture.) The first resurrection is a very select governing group, caught up to be with Christ in his throne in heaven. Numerically, it is precisely defined by God only. It is *"a great multitude, which no man can number."* No man can number or definitively qualify those "Elect Saints." The *"great multitude"* is the same Greek expression as used in Matthew 26:47. It did not mean an insurmountable number. It meant a body of people of purpose. Positionally, they are at the Throne of God. They are Celestials and they are *"of all nations, and kindreds, and people, and tongues."* God loves diversity. His preference reflects diversity.

Timewise, the seventh chapter is bounded by the ended fifth seal, Revelation 6:11, and the beginning of the seventh seal, Revelation 8:1. The more precise time, a limited and horrific period, would be the sixth seal, a World War. The *"supper"* aspect would extend thru the continued time of warring and *"vials"* until Armageddon. That celebratory or victory supper may occupy seven-and-a-half years.

The seventh chapter is important because it gives the estate of God's chosen, both terrestrial and celestial. The 144,000 Celestials of the first resurrection are caught up to the throne of God in Revelation 12:5. They are with Christ in rulership and set to witness the wrath of God on the ungodly. The 144,000 terrestrial Jews are sealed and poised to head the government of God on earth. God is now beginning to completely fulfill all the promises made to Abraham. That would be all the promises concerning natural Israel. Many promises relate to the geography of the Middle East, and touch the matter of *"Hephzibah, and thy land Beulah: for the Lord delighteth in thee, and thy land shall be married"* (Isaiah 62:4). That well qualifies as a "bride message" pertaining to the natural Jew: the people, blessed of God, married to the land.

Revelation 7:1–3

"Four angels standing on the four corners of the earth, holding the four winds of the earth, that the wind should not blow on the earth, nor on the sea, nor on any tree. And I saw another angel ascending from the east, having the seal

of the living God: and he cried with a loud voice to the four angels, to whom it was given to hurt the earth and the sea, Saying, <u>Hurt not the earth, neither the sea, not the trees, till we have sealed the servants of our God in their foreheads.*</u>

The word *till* above may not be the same Greek word as *until* in 6:11, but it carries the same meaning and it refers to the same time frame of three-and-a-half years.

At the time of the command *"Hurt not"* it is assumed they had not yet hurt the earth or the sea. However, they had hurt the earth and the sea to a one-third degree. Beyond that, even the heavens were affected. It was a command to stop hurting and give space. What space? Till the servants of our God were sealed. The sealing was accomplished during the fifth seal, and the conclusion of the matter was marked by the sixth seal, a World War. Ungodly man continued hurting the chosen and the sealed with his vindications and wrath. The fifth seal was a time, three-and-a-half years of martyrdom. That time of the <u>wrath of man and demons</u> was a precursor to the beginning of the seventh seal and the <u>wrath of God</u> poured out from heaven. The seventh seal was *"silence in heaven"* and hell on earth for seven-and-a-half years. In Revelation 8:1, then 10:1–7, 11:15–19, and 15:1–16:21, including the conclusion, Armageddon was overshadowed by God's final cleansing righteous wrath.

The *catching away*, or rapture, of the man child is on the front end of the seven-and-a-half years wrath of God. In that sense, we believe in a "pre-Tribulation" rapture. However, the *catching away*, or rapture, is preceded by three-and-a-half years wrath of man and then three-and-a-half years wrath of man and demons. Those first two quarters, totaling seven years, are also a time of tribulation, but not the specified wrath of God. Looking at the timeline with a greater light of understanding, we may be considered "mid-Tribulation" believers. In the overview, it's like Paul said, *"We have no such custom."* Call it, "no such traditional teaching."

A related point of understanding: The catching away marks the beginning of the millennium reign of Christ. It also marks the beginning of the time of the wrath of God. That would be the time of seven thunders and seven vials. This seven-and-a-half-year period of time is on the front end of the one thousand years and going forward seven-and-a-half years into the millennium. The basis is this: The type or similitude of Abraham (God) and Isaac (Christ) and Eliezer (Holy Ghost) and Rebecca (Bride) and, lastly, Sara's tent located in Hebron (heaven). The event of the marriage was in Hebron. As per that similitude, the marriage supper of the Lamb is in heaven. It is an extended supper ending with Armageddon. Following the type: King David (type of Christ) reigned in Hebron for seven-and-a-half years before he took Jerusalem. That seven-and-a-half years was part of his forty-year reign. The similitude says that the marriage supper of the Lamb, or the time of the seated-in-heaven begins the one thousand years as did King David's reign in Hebron. The enlightenment is: The reign of Christ begins at the time of the rapture and the seven-and-a-half years of wrath leading up to Armageddon is in the first seven-and-a-half years of the millennium. In other words, Armageddon is seven-and-a-half years into the seventh day.

It might be a help to some if 8:1 was attached immediately after 6:17. Thus, 8:2 would be the more obvious beginning verse of chapter 8. Revelation 8:2 is a time-restart that connects back to the starting time of 6:1. To wit: Revelation 6:1–17 is the heavenly perspective and directive. Revelation 8:2–9:21 treats the same time frame and sequence of events, but it is reflecting the *"cast it into the earth"* (Revelation 8:5). That is how it was to be accomplished in the earth.

Going forward into the seventh day or the "Lord's Day" or the thousand-year day, there will be multitudes resurrected. Those will be, for the most part, raised to go on unto overcomer status. Unless they are resurrected and living at the closing of that one-thousand-year day they will live out their lives and die. Not a problem; faith abounds and the parting will be a sort of "see you later." Reasonably, life-spans will increase as the one thousand years progress. Death will be in unity with a reward written and sealed in heaven. Jesus told Martha, *"I am the resurrection, and the life."* It is a "given" that his seventh day would be a thousand-year day of resurrection.

The second or final resurrection is at the end of one thousand years. Specifically, it happens early in the eighth day. For those just mentioned, who are passed on having been granted <u>everlasting life</u>, it will be a literal resurrection, and it will include <u>terrestrials</u> only. For those who are alive at the time and have gained that victory, it is the time of transitioning from transient lives to eternal life. That is a sort of resurrection from transient to never die again, possibly even an immediate reversal of their ageing process." Hopefully, the total of the living that are changed and those literally resurrected will number in the untold millions.

With that baseline, we can better identify the first group of 144,000 in Revelation 7:4–8, and then the second group, Revelation 7:9–17. The second group being *"these which are arrayed in white robes."* In the overview, we see more clearly the purpose and time placement of chapter 7.

Spirit, Soul, and Body

1 Thessalonians 5:23—*"And the very God of peace sanctify you wholly; and I pray God your whole* **spirit** *and* **soul** *and* **body** *be preserved blameless unto the coming of our Lord Jesus Christ."*

THE PLAN OF GOD treats mankind as foremost and primary. Studying the components of man, created by God, that facilitated sin and orchestrates his redemption is a need to know. That is the reason this chapter is written. It is an addendum to an earlier section on the subject: Spirit (*pneuma*), soul (*psyche*), and body (*soma*). Again, many of the statements and principles have been expressed in earlier sections. Even so, a knowledge of the detail of how God deals with a person's individuality and makeup is necessary. No apology is offered for requesting the reader's indulgence.

The teachings on this subject are of old, going back to the time of the early church fathers. To expound on the several viewpoints would be beyond the scope of this writing. This writer does not treat the subject as mere knowledge or as a doctrine; rather, we hold that the understanding is revealing and helpful toward a better grasp of God's way and means to accomplish his intent.

The subject, correctly taught, offers an excellent baseline for teaching the three realms as it pertains to the creation and the individual. Specifically, the belief that man is a tripartite being; spirit, soul, and body. Again, this entry may be considered a postscript to earlier sections of this book. However, beyond that, it includes added thoughts and further understanding of man's fall and God's provision for restoration.

Introducing the Basic Parameters Regarding This Subject

Presently, there exist three realms. First, the Spirit realm (Creator), and second, the material, natural, or physical realm (creation). Thirdly, there exist the living creation, inclusive of both animal and plant life. The highest of this order was man. At whatever instant he was God-connected, there came to be another realm; the psychological or psyche realm (the "in God's image" creature). It should be obvious that the three realms underlined above equate to spirit, body, and soul, respectively.

Repeating: The Spirit realm is what and where God is. As Paul said in Ephesians 4:6, *"One God and Father of all, who is above all, and through all, and in you all."* The material or physical realm was a subsequent realm brought into existence by God. The observable material realm exists, as do all things, within the Spirit realm.

God created the plant and animal kingdoms and spoke life into them. More explicitly; God transformed inanimate material into mechanisms that received and perpetuated natural life. Animals think and have thinking processes, but that thinking is not connected to God beyond relating to the natural habitat and to God's other creatures. As such, they fall into the category of creation creatures. Of all the creatures, only mankind was created with God's intent of being spiritually connected to himself, Spirit. Call it at-one-ment of spirits.

Genesis 2:7 states, *"And the Lord God formed man of the dust of the ground* (body), *and breathed into his nostrils the breath of life* (spirit); *and man became a living soul* (soul)." To wit: God made the body or tabernacle of a to-be-living soul. Then he breathed life, Spirit, into that body and it became a living soul, a thinking being. At that point, Adam, like the animals, was a product and representative of two realms. Reasonably, man had superior thinking or processing of thought beyond the animal kingdom. However, without the God-connection he would be, categorically, just part of the creation. Scripture does not define as to whether man was immediately God-connected as Spirit–spirit at the time of his creation physiologically, but he certainly was at the time God placed him in the Garden of Eden. As such, he was a soul that constituted a third realm, the psychological realm. The psychological, or thought, realm exists within the Spiritual realm. Man was created to thoughtfully subordinate to the Spirit realm. He was in obedience to his creator. Thinking man, being self, the person, has *freedom of will,* the capability of obedience or otherwise provoke God, suffering separation. Again, Adam was created and placed in Eden with the blessed estate of being in the image of God. He was creative and he had freedom of choice. *"And God saw every thing that he had made, and, behold it was very good"* (Genesis 1:31).

Adam and Eve did sin and did suffer separation. Since Eden was that place of unity with God, they were cast out and thus fell to a lesser place in God's creation. Solomon's Ecclesiastes, in parts, has the flavor of a man that sorrows as one whose spirit is separated from the Spirit of God. It is as if man, in his portrayal, has slipped to the estate of the animal kingdom.

Adam was created and placed in Eden with the blessed estate of being in the image of God. He was creative and he had freedom of choice. *"And God saw every thing that he had made, and, behold it was very good"* (Genesis 1:31). Creativity is good and freedom to choose is good, but if an evil inspiration enters and corrupts, those innate gifts and capabilities, be it usurpation from without or purely from within the realm of man's doings, it is evil. Henceforth, it is man's creation of a contrary nature. His spirit was no longer at-one-ment with God, a Spirit, and Adam's psyche realm (soul) was reduced to the estate of *"enmity."* Man was separated unto his world of iniquity where death was the reward. It can rightfully be termed the "first heaven," born of sin. It was a separated estate, heaven, and it was man's creation. Legally, it would be "a creation of the state." That is, the state of sin, and, as such, it is an "unnatural body." It was a fall from God's prescribed order of the realms: Firstly, preeminent Spirit–spirit of man. Secondly, the obedient thinking, reasoning man, soul. Thirdly, the body suborning and without the prerogative of "demand." Again, that is true at-one-ment.

Tripartite Man

As relating to the tripartite nature of man, it is our benefit, even a spiritual need, that we gain sufficient understanding of the subject. It shines light on the born-again Christian's benefitting operation of the Spirit of God alive and effectual in their life. Such an interest and searching for truth is necessary toward the healing of a blind spot. The blind spot is to say that the spirit of a man is problematic, even categorically evil, as if our spirit is "a bad spirit." If our thinking on the subject stops there that would be a dreadful blind spot.

Please let me refresh a few points. Prior to the advent of man, God had already created living creatures but they related only to the material natural realm, having no capacity to commune, be led, or have conscience toward God. Unlike animals, man has God-given communion, sensitivity of conscience, and intuition which equates to a spiritually ordained dominion. With Adam, it was dominion over the creation. With us, it is dominion over the world, the flesh, and the devil. Before the Fall, Adam was God-connected as a spiritual, physical being. After the Fall, Adam was disconnected spiritually and having been expelled from the Garden of Eden, he lost communion with God, sensitivity of conscience toward God, and, more obviously, he lost dominion. Having known the "God connection," and then being void of that, has to be the greatest sorrow imaginable. Could it be that when God *"made him to be sin for us, who knew no sin"* (2 Corinthians 5:21); that is, on the cross, suffering death in our stead, Jesus felt that separation and cried out, *"My God, my God why has thou forsaken me?"* (Matthew 27:46).

Now, thru the precious saving blood of Jesus Christ, we are reconnected. Romans 8:15, 16, states, *"Ye have received the Spirit of adoption, whereby we cry, Abba, Father. The* <u>Spirit</u> *itself beareth witness with our* <u>spirit</u>*, that we are the children of God."* Paul said the same in 1 Corinthians 6:17, *"But he that is joined unto the Lord is one* <u>spirit</u>*."* Ideally, the spirit of man responds to the Spirit realm. The soul, as defined, functions in the psychological or thinking realm. The body functions in the material or physical realm. God relates to man by the Spirit–spirit connection. *"The Lord weigheth the spirits"* (Proverbs 16:2). Rarely did God relate to man on a conscious, psyche, level. In such cases, it was a marker of their special status. Moses and Christ had that extraordinary experience. They were <u>Apostles of God</u>. The Early Rain Apostles had that experience as Christ appeared to them after his Ascension from the Mount of Olives. They were <u>Apostles of Christ</u>.

Any affinity to God, who is Spirit, would be thru the connected spirit in man. That connection is not directly with the natural reasoning "person," or "soul" (psyche). The connection is thru the Spirit (Pneuma) to spirit (pneuma) connection. Knowing this will result in a proper valuing of the spirit of man. Getting past a blind spot, we can fully understand Paul's statement in 1 Thessalonians 5:23, *"And the very God of peace sanctify you wholly; and I pray God your whole spirit* (pneuma) *and soul* (psyche) *and body* (soma) *be preserved blameless unto the coming of our Lord Jesus Christ."* Jude 1 uses the same phrase, *"preserved in Jesus Christ, and called."* The preservation of the whole person lies in the maintaining of a right order. To wit: The Spirit is in the lead and preeminent, and the person, or soul, is subject to the Spirit leading, whereas the body is "under" and has no right of demand. As Paul said, *"But I keep* <u>under</u> *my body, and bring it into subjection: lest that by any means, when I have preached to others, I myself should be a castaway"* (1 Corinthians 9:27). Right order: That is our covering. That is our preservation.

Simply put, right order is Spirit–spirit, soul, body. Wrong order is body, soul, spirit-disconnect. Man was created in the image of God and he abode in the "estate" of obedience and innocence. That place was prepared of God and it was "Eden." Sin entered and man fell to the state of disobedience and guilt. That is the fallen estate of Adam's creation; mankind's first heaven. A kind of "corporation." That is, the state's creation of an "unnatural body." Again, the estate of sin and death.

The question has been raised as to whether sin entered the garden because of, or by way of, <u>sensual sin</u> (body), <u>disobedience</u> (soul/psyche), or pride-driven <u>unbelief</u> (spiritual offence). The fact is that all three were in play. The next question: How would the "Adversary" enter the picture? How would a "Serpent" take advantage? The answer: The low way. First, the natural physical body was stirred up to do a fleshly act against God's will and plan. Then the soul, or thinking part, yielded in disobedience. This cast the whole of the person into pride-driven unbelief and idolatry. The result was a disconnect of Spirit (God) with man's spirit. Man fell to the estate of sin and death. At that point, the ruling order became body, soul, and the spirit under. That would be, man came under flesh or creature rule. In a similitude, circumcision became uncircumcision.

Romans 1:21–25 reveals the fallen estate as it developed and was addressed by the apostle Paul in his time among the Romans. *"Because that, when they knew God, they glorified him not as God, neither were thankful; but became vain in their imaginations, and their foolish heart was darkened. Professing themselves to be wise, they became fools, And changed the glory of the uncorruptible God into an image made like to corruptible man, and to birds, and four-footed beast, and creeping things (idolatry). Wherefore God also gave them up to uncleanness through the lust of their own hearts, to dishonour their own bodies between themselves: Who changed the truth of God into a lie, and worshipped and served the creature more than the Creator, who is blessed for ever. Amen."* (pride-driven idolatry)

That battle rages: *"The flesh lusteth against the Spirit, and the Spirit against the flesh: and these are contrary the one to the other"* (Galatians 5:17). Worshiping the creation is not good. Worshiping the creature is definitely not good. Similarly; being servant to the creation is not good and serving the creature is definitely not good. Again, idolatry.

The victory is the Lord's, and it is ours. Overcoming and perfection is the same as accomplishing God's perfect order. In this section of writing, that applies to the order of the individual's life. In the bigger picture it applies to all of creation.

Chart and Explanation with Intended Redundancy

Relating to the grand scheme of things, and for the purpose of clarifying the abovementioned overturning, let us consider: The <u>Creator is Spirit,</u> the <u>Creature is Soul,</u> and the <u>Creation is Body</u>. Thus, let a few comparisons be set forth.

Man, as an individual, has three components. <u>He has a spiritual part (spirit)</u> that communes with Spirit-God. <u>He has a thinking part (soul)</u> that is connected to God through his spiritual part, and that thinking part also communicates with the world, or creation, around him. <u>He has a physical part (body)</u>, and, in a bodily sense, he is part of creation. He is the creature.

1 Thessalonians 5:23	<u>Spirit</u> (Pneuma) Creator–Creature	<u>Soul</u> (psyche) Creature	<u>Body</u> (soma) Creation
Mankind as Created	The Spirit was pre-eminent and leading in man.	The thinking man was subject to the Creator.	The physical part was subordinate.

Satanic influence comes in the *low way*, that is, via the unthinking body/soma, and sets forth fleshly or sarx drives. These work on the psyche of man and turn him toward disobedience. After all, *"The serpent was more subtle than any beast of the field which the LORD GOD had made."* That new drive of the flesh and the resulting flesh-driven creature moved Adam to disobey God's commandment. He subordinated the spiritual man, moving him toward unbelief. Thus, instead of a spirit–soul–body ordered person, Adam became a perverted order; body–soul–spirit person. Mankind was, from that fallen state forward, subordinate, and in service, to the creature rather than the Creator. Perverted sensual desire, disobedience, and the resulting unbelief; <u>all</u> were in play in the sin in the garden.

Sin Yielded:	Spirit: <u>Unbelief</u> (Devil, Satan)	Soul: <u>Disobedience</u> (Dragon, Satan)	Body: <u>Sensual</u> (Serpent, Satan)
The World	Pride of Life	Lust of the Eye	Lust of the Flesh
Lost:	Life/Conscience	"Son" Status/ Communion	Intuition/Dominion
Price:	Enmity/Death/Hell	War/Sword	Famine/Pestilence

CHAPTER 8

Troubling Issues Clouding the Light of Truth

Treating the Impossible: Necessary Change of Hearts and Minds

THIS SECTION ADDRESSES SEVERAL subjects. Some are controversial. Some are latent-explosive. They could be termed "hot spots" on the religious docket. These doctrinal hot spots may also have the ominous rank of erroneous, or at least lacking the whole truth. I use the term "blind spots."

This discussion of "issues" is not off subject to the Plan of God. The whole matter relates to our embrace and the "spirit" we hold and reflect of the "Plan of God." Our embrace of God's plan is our "vision."

Failing to discern a blind spot will hinder the more complete understanding of a critical precept. How great is that loss if we fail to gain truth in an ongoing fashion, even the whole truth of a principal precept? God's provision for his people is to grant them the necessary understanding of present knowledge. *Spiritual blindness*, or blind spot, is not always a case of failed intellect. The more critical question, is it a matter of callousness of spirit? In other terminology, we might say that a blind spot is carnality, and circumcision of the heart is much needed. The most dreadful feature of a blind spot is marginalizing the cost of resting in our carnality. Breaking free of any lifelong comfort zone requires a spiritual quickening.

I trust that the reader knows what we are talking about. If not, then let them be informed that there are numerous fractures in the religious doctrinal landscape. The heartbeat of this section of the book is to realize that fact, address some of those schisms, and then pray the Holy Ghost will facilitate the path to get it right. The reader may find the following subjects are a combination of mind-bending and irritating. The primary concern here is that we not become "mean-spirited," or call a cessation to the whole of the desire and effort to get it right.

We know that only God can change a person's mind. I prayed for the Lord's help in writing this book and now I pray for the Lord's help toward the reader. Otherwise, without God's gift of desire and patience, the reading will end shortly. As a word of encouragement: Embrace a good spiritual diet, so that you *"may know to refuse the evil, and choose the good."*

This section is lengthy. Some aspects of the subject material have been mentioned already. Your indulgence is requested. The desire toward you is that you not cast away the good understanding you presently possess. However, it may involve the Lord's leading toward a willingness to add further understanding to an issue you thought to be complete and settled. For all that: "Don't throw the baby out with the bathwater."

The reading is profitable if it speaks to the need for change, a change of mind which is necessary to open doors of knowledge. Don't fear as though you are compromising your loyalties. The greater fear must be that we lack the humility to change. Paul stated, *"We have received, not the spirit of the world, but the spirit which is of God; that we might know the things that are freely given to us of God"* (1 Corinthians 2:12). Godly understanding enters thru the door of humility and confession. In the world of politics, no one gives up their "schedule." This is not politics.

The requirement for settlement, in matters of doctrinal disputes, is found in the register of things we do not know and not in declaring, even boasting, of the things that we do know.

Humbling as it may be, we need to keep that fact in mind when we approach differences that come to bear in doctrinal discussions. We reasonably determine that both sides cannot be altogether right, but both sides can be wrong. A liberal stance may say that both understandings are right and the difference is primarily a matter of semantics. Fervent argument and contending for the truth will not allow this sort of concession. Typically, we see both sides having sufficient truth to persist with a kind of immunity, at least to the point of a no settlement, thus, departing back to a particular school of thought, with adherents. In the overview, any such closure is not an acceptable ending. We are hard pressed to allow any "out" for missing the mark (sin) in matters that address our eternal salvation, or even our relationship with the Lord and his people. That touches the basic premise of loving God and loving others.

A realistic "knowing" necessarily moves us to prioritize the need for togetherness. Sometimes, we grudgingly reconcile; convinced that avoiding dissention and division is preferable and more beneficial than a dogged pursuit of our viewpoint. Charitable, yes; but again, that is not an ideal or acceptable ending. Relating to the teaching realm, this is where many find themselves. It has been said, "The further you go into religious disputes the deeper it gets." So be it, but we do have a baseline concerning truth that remains absolute, and that is to be Spirit-led. That is not a trite or juvenile approach. The often-missing element is God-ordained, Spirit-led Ministry. The desired estate for the Church includes love for his Ministry, togetherness, and agreement. The avenue to unity, in matters of doctrine, is a Spirit-led Leadership who are *"endeavouring to keep the unity of the Spirit in the bond of peace . . . Till we all come in the unity of the faith, and of the knowledge of the Son of God, unto a perfect man, unto the measure of the stature of the fullness of Christ"* (Ephesians 4:3, 13).

Regarding patience: Waiting on the dispensation of greater authority, and at the time of the Lord's choosing, is God's more perfect will. He is the Head of the Church. *"In your patience possess ye your souls"* (Luke 21:19). Suffice to say, doctrine is serious business, with great demand for correctness or correction. We humbly confess that the great prerequisite for gaining deeper truths and settlements is to have patience with a willingness to embrace; "more of Him and less of me." And then *let patience have her perfect work, that ye may be perfect and entire, wanting nothing*" (James 1:4). Keep in mind that *"the trying of your faith worketh patience*" (James 1:3).

Regarding repentance: *"My little children, these things write I unto you, that ye sin not. And if any man sin, we have an advocate with the Father, Jesus Christ the righteous*" (1 John 2:1). Thankfully, we have this saving grace offered by our forgiving Lord. However, treating the matter of teaching or contending for truth, we may not be inclined to embrace our Lord's forgiveness. Reason: Doctrinal disputes usually include the matter of personal standing, reputation, and a person's perceived spiritual estate. On that point, timing is important. Our delivery of an insight, even profound truth, may be premature. The act of repentance, from a repentant spirit, is always in order when we venture into revelation, where we know and express godly fear: "It is as dark a mile ahead of God as it is a mile behind God."

Regarding unity: Consensus is hoped for, even presently lacking gifted authorities. To wit: The fullness of a fivefold gifted ministry, especially the Apostle, Prophet, and Teacher. On that point, looking back to the Early Rain, we see ministers who were less than perfect having "Apostle" status. That should give us pause, considering the possibility of the near move of God toward ordination of such an authority. Settlement of doctrinal disputes would be forthcoming.

We must *"esteem other better than ourselves*" (Philippians 2:3). This humility of mind and spirit is the avenue through which God works to enlighten his elect. Lacking this fruit is not only a blind spot, but it will ferment and perpetuate greater error. Humility and contriteness of heart is the channel through which the Lord brings truth and unity. Truly, these are the earmarks of citizenship for the new heaven and new earth. This fruit of the Spirit, manifested in a person, will often result in others talking down to them and counting them out of the teaching rank of the Church. Maintaining integrity in this testing will reveal authenticity verses guile because the carnal man will not tolerate being marginalized or ignored. Bottom line: Love God and love others better than yourself, all the while maintaining integrity. Forfeit your agenda. Net product: Unity.

Regarding the seriousness of repeating or teaching doctrinal error: A reasonable disclaimer is that a person qualifies their teaching with the statement, "This is the way our organization's founding fathers taught it." If there is a lack of personal revelation, treating the subject at hand, such a disclaimer has validity. Not validity as to correctness of teaching but validity in turning away the reproach of error. We often correctly discern the spirit of a Bible teacher as honestly presenting their teaching of doctrine as proceeding from themselves. They are "professing," and the highest order of "Teacher" is the "Professor." Preferably, doctrinal teaching would proceed from such a right-spirited Holy Ghost-connected teacher. Short of godly inspiration, a book-report delivery is rarely esteemed or even acceptable with a listening spirit-filled Church.

The Body of Christ, whatever its estate, has primary and established truth: truth that is foundational, unchanging, and resident. Furthermore, on the *"yea, yea"* side, we do entertain the prospect of fully ordained apostolic gifts. The recipients would have Jesus appear to them on a conscious level, not a dream or vision.

Until then, the Lord requires his children be thankful and not as those *"who hath despised the day of small things"* (Zechariah 4:10). That knowledge and attitude could help open the door to usher in the fullness of the Lord's end-time church administration. In that fullness, an apostolic ministry would orchestrate the settlement of doctrinal differences that concern God's people. We are rightfully building on *"the foundation of the apostles and prophets, Jesus Christ himself being the chief corner stone"* (Ephesians 2:20).

A related similitude meant to encourage us: At the sea of Tiberias, John 21:1, 2, Thomas (Didymus, a twin, ditto) and other six were witness to Jesus' presence for the third time. Of the seven, Peter was mentioned first and then Thomas. Peter was representative of the early church foundation of apostles, Thomas represented the latter church. The point being: Look at the picture and see that Thomas knew but he did not know that he knew. Jesus said, *"And whither I go ye know, and the way ye know. Thomas saith unto him, Lord, we know not whither thou goest; and how can we know the way?"* (John 14:4, 5). We are to exhort one another *"to earnestly contend for the faith which was once delivered unto the saints"* (Jude 3).

In matters of doctrinal change or refinements, we exercise fear of God and carefulness. Basic biblical truths are precious and God-given for our very salvation. While giving place to such carefulness, we should likewise concern ourselves with that great library of error left standing because of the fear of violating the statutes. Fearing man is real and reasonable, but fearing God should be preeminent.

A Review

Failing to realize the foibles and pitfalls, in adding understanding to our present knowledge, constitute blind spots. The requirement for a settlement, in matters of dispute, is often found in the register of things we don't know and not in declaring the things that we do know. Both sides cannot be right and without error; but, both sides can be wrong, both having error.

The prerequisite for gaining deeper truths, settlements, and the dispensing of any gift is to have patience, the right spirit, and a willingness to act charitably with obvious civility.

Treating the matter of repentance (changing) when teaching or contending for truth: When in error, we may not be inclined to embrace, in humility, our Lord's forgiveness. That would be a blind spot with dreadful personal consequence. Past leadership, if they were on station now, would repent or concede certain points and going forward, would make changes for the benefit of a more complete and accurate understanding. Entrenchment in the past would cast us as aligning with the most truth-limiting and destructive earmark of organization. A living tree, cut down and shaped, will never again grow and produce fruit.

We do see apostolic gifts among us, past and present, but not in the fullness of the Early Rain Church dispensation. That very confession could open the doors that would help usher in the fullness of the Lord's Church administration, the gifts. Therein resides the final and complete settlement of doctrinal differences that presently concern God's people. Truth is present, but the settlement of some aspects of that truth, and the disposing of error, requires apostolic authority.

The ideal end point of any contest is that an advocate of some doctrine will have a spirit of thankfulness, repentance, forgiveness, worship, and the fear of God. Actually, more than just an ideal, these attributes are required. Also, concurrently and always in order: A declaration of the desire for truth, above and beyond personal exaltation. We need not only hear that declaration, but feel and know, in our spirit, the accompanying humility of heart.

The discussion of difficult doctrinal divides necessitates we see honest confession that our insights and comments will not exhaust the subjects nor reflect infallibility.

This writer's hope is that blind spots can be helped and divisions healed. Again, with all that being expressed: Lord, heal my blind spots. Lord, help your people surmount any offence, especially in the face of greater truth, so that no person be left behind, blinded by prejudice.

Troubling Issues Worthy of Consideration
(Matters of Contest and Possibly Unpleasant Topics)

The list: Time and Space, Duality of Interpretation, The Man–Child Message, Spirit–Soul–Body, Moving Out Alive, Restoration of the Jew, The End-Time Message, Pre-, Mid-, or Post -Tribulation Rapture? Organization, The Mortality of the Soul, and The Godhead. Those subjects are enumerated because of the historical cessation of added revelation that could have more clearly defined the issues. Beyond the *"seem to come short of it"* factor is doctrinal prejudice and a clouding of a clear focus of God's plan. This book will not begin to move weighty mainstream thought and rooted doctrines. It is a torrential force, and it is peculiar to the way mankind behaves. Our expression of hope is that greater revelation would overtake blind spots, and even overturn error. That could only happen if God ordains it so, and when he directs that His Word light the subject.

This writing thus far seems to addresses matters having to do with the Church. Esoteric. The writer's thoughts and concerns reach beyond like-minded believers, and include various schools of thought; especially accepted secular–religious orthodoxy and mainline organization. Call that part an exoteric mandate. This writing should reflect a "knowing," according to the similitudes given by Jesus: The Kingdom is not only *"his garner,"* it is also likened to a *"net."*

This section will certainly demonstrate that this book and this writer are not part or party to any higher teaching magisterium. And, it is unlikely this sole cry for change will move the needle. Nevertheless, we have the right to hope that schools of great learning and higher orders will eventually review and ameliorate some concepts.

Two "troubling" issues are left unattended in this section: Calvinism's particular treatment of predestination and the question of the Devil, as an individuality or Evil, as the Devil, being conceptual. The devil issue has its "settlement" in the arena of "origins" and that touches an area "off the table." See introduction and chapter IV. Both issues are respectfully mentioned ongoing earlier in the book.

The space given to each of the items varies. The purpose is to encourage thoughtful considerations; if not to many, at least to the individual.

Time and Space

We think of phenomena such as time, the universe, unending space, and eternity as overriding, preeminent concepts. That is, we think that Almighty God is somehow within those parameters. We've heard the statement, "God is somewhere out there." Not so. God is beyond any parameters or infinite space or anything else we can bend our mind around. We might venture to say he has a "point of emanation." We do well to pass on a temptation to go beyond that, lest we end up attempting to "qualify" God's omnipresence. The arguments of science are weighty and the nomenclature overwhelming, maybe falling into the category of *"oppositions of science falsely so called"* (1 Timothy 6:20).

A comic made the statement that "time was nature's way of keeping everything from happening at the same time." Everybody laughed. The statement was laughable, and it was meant to be comical, because time takes precedence over nature. Nature is subordinate to time. I'm not sure an understanding audience would laugh if it was said, "Time is God's only way of keeping everything from happening at the same time." To the point: God is not subordinate to time or space. To believe this does not require being learned or having special knowledge. Admittedly, we do not understand the mechanics of the Spirit Realm. Not possible. What we can do, and what we need to do forthwith, is eliminate this blind spot and confess to an earlier quote. *"One God and Father of all, who is above all, and through all, and in you all."* Also, Ephesians 4:6. God *"calleth those things which be not as though they were"* (Romans 4:17).

If he so ordains, we can gain the high ground of understanding His Plan. And that will happen, in an increasing manner, as we increase in confession, humility, and revelation: all prerequisite to God shining a light which heals our blind spots.

This understanding, or better said, "confession," gives us a very necessary basis to correctly view prophecy and predestination. It may be most helpful in understanding the advent of Christ and the nature of his individuality, in the very beginning, with the Father, before the world was.

Duality of Interpretation

Solomon stated in Proverbs 25:2, *"It is the glory of God to conceal a thing: but the honor of kings is to search out a matter."* Relating to duality of interpretation, I'll mention a few instances, some obvious and some not-so-obvious. The hope is to demonstrate the fact that spiritual discernment is helpful toward gaining knowledge, and then the understanding of God's Plan and Intent. Most people, even serious students, are put off by what seems to be error or confusion in the narrative. Thus, the thing is hidden.

Hosea 11:1 stated, *"When Israel was a child, then I loved him, and called my son out of Egypt."* Over seven hundred years later, Matthew 2:15 reads, *"That it might be fulfilled which was spoken of the Lord by the prophet, saying, Out of Egypt have I called my son."* Both Hosea and Matthew, if they could have talked, would likely have said: We're both right. End of conversation. That kind of settlement would reflect a different phrase, *duality of facts.* Not to be marginalizing an important prophecy, but we are sometimes seeing double when Scripture, especially prophecy, is meant to be coincidental, even if set in different time frames.

Let's look at Daniel 12:4, *"But thou, O Daniel, shut up the words, and seal the book, even to the time of the end: many shall run to and fro, and knowledge shall be increased."* That does depict this present world. However, knowledge also increased in Jesus' time or era. The bedrock of considerable science, philosophical, and societal thinking was set forth by Greek and Roman proponents, and, people and armies of the day were on the move. Admittedly, it looks like that description best fits our present era. Since we are eyes on, the statements do, for us, fit exactly. Stopping with that prognosis is a no-settlement conclusion. Going forward:

Consider that *"the time of the end,"* verse 4 mentioned above, keys on verses 6 and 7: *"How long shall it be to the end of these wonders . . . it shall be for* <u>a time, times, and an half</u>*"* This reference is an exact fit to the last half of Daniel's seventieth week mentioned in Daniel 9:27. Right here, we'll bring in a parallel: Revelation 12:13, 14. *"And when the dragon saw that he was cast unto the earth, he persecuted the woman which brought forth the man child. And to the woman were given two wings of a great eagle, that she might fly into the wilderness, into her place, where she is nourished for* <u>a time, and times, and half a time</u>*, from the face of the serpent."* Both these three-and-a-half year periods are coincidental in the most amazing way; a sort of duality. Believing God's amazing and encompassing truth toward accomplishing his will, we see a duality of fulfillment. Explanation: Four scriptural interpretations will be brought to bear. First, Micah 5:3: *"Therefore will he give them up, until the time that she which travaileth hath brought forth: then the remnant of his brethren shall return unto the children of Israel."* This *"give them up"* refers to the two thousand years *"great gulf"* of Luke 16:26, starting with the fulfillment of the seventy weeks of Daniel 9:24–27, then onward *"until the time that* <u>she which travaileth</u> <u>hath brought forth.</u>*"* That is the same event as Revelation 12:2, 5. *"And she being with child cried, travailing in birth, and pain to be delivered . . . And* <u>she brought forth</u> *a man child, who was to rule all nations with a rod of iron: and her child was* <u>caught up</u> *unto God, and to his throne."* The *"caught up"* is the catching away, or rapture, of the *"man child,"* later depicted as the bride, the Lamb's wife.

For the sake of adding clarification: The catching away ends the production of the two-thousand-year church, *"she,"* age. It begins the seventh day, being Christ's rule. The Gentile era is over. The sun goes down for them and rises for the Jew. The Jew is inclusive of all mankind that embraces the Lord Jesus, being sons of Abraham by faith. That is important to know; yes, vital that you understand that fact. The 144,000 terrestrial Jewish vanguard leadership comes into function.

The two thousand years' time frame is equal to the time of the Gentiles. If the time is prophetically rendered as the Jew's dead time, that time gulf is nonexistent for the Jew. It, the two thousand years, goes away and the last half of the seventieth week of Daniel 9:27 is brought up to connect and overlap the end of the last three-and-a-half years of the Gentile times. As per Isaiah 21:12, *"The watchman said, The morning cometh, and also the night: if ye will inquire, enquire ye: return, come."* The last three-and-a-half year period before the catching away of the very elect, or man–child, is coincidental to the sealing of the 144,000 Jews of Revelation 7. The morning comes to the Jew but at the same time it is a sun going down for the Gentiles.

The "Man Child" Message: Revelation 7:9–17, 12:5, 14:1

This section will add insight to the revelation of God's plan. The criteria, *"man child"* falls within the subject of "resurrection." The subject is deserving of repetition. The following statements are meant to introduce, engage, and then encourage the reader toward agreement to the actuality of a definitive 144,000-person "catching away." Again, this discussion is somewhat repetitive, but the further treatment is warranted, with an awareness that it is fitting for this chapter on "Troubling Issues."

Greater knowledge of the resurrection will necessarily include the more detailed understanding of the first and second or final resurrection. The first resurrection might be thought of as a "select rapture." That resurrection feature is scriptural, and it is doctrinally correct. Without that knowledge, the resurrection event, as often portrayed, is chaotic and stretches the imagination. It generates great emotion, and it is engaging, even entertaining. That scenario, as brought forth, is thought-provoking but it is not a true reflection of God's order and the way he does things. Those who gain the truth on this subject are a minority.

Note: If the reader's understanding of resurrection differs from this presentation, know that there is no intent to marginalize your viewpoint.

(Revelation 7:1–8 gives time, allowance, and place to the 144,000 terrestrial Jews that will be set forward as the "earthly" component in the time frame of the "catching away." They are not the primary object of this section/explanation.)

Revelation 7:9–17: This second group of chapter 7 are the ascended *"man child"* or the *"caught up"* ones (Revelation 12:5). They are the 144,000 of Revelation 14:1. These are the first Resurrection Saints, Elect of God. They later appear, after the seventh one thousand years, as *"descending out of heaven from God"* (Revelation 21:10). They are then called *"the bride, the Lamb's wife"* (Revelation 21:9).

The first resurrection is from mortal to <u>immortal</u> and from terrestrial to <u>celestial</u>. It is limited to the 144,000 chosen of God. (For starters, we can reference 1 Corinthians 15:40, then forward with other Scripture.) The first resurrection is a very select governing group, caught up to be with Christ in his throne in heaven for one thousand years. Numerically, it is precisely defined <u>by God only</u>. It is *"a great multitude, which <u>no man can number</u>."* No man can number or definitively qualify those "Elect Saints." The *"great multitude"* is the same Greek expression as used in Matthew 26:47. It did not mean an insurmountable number. It means "a body of people of purpose." Positionally, they are at the Throne of God. They are Celestials and they are *"of all nations, and kindreds, and people, and tongues."* God loves diversity. His preference reflects diversity.

Timewise, the seventh chapter is bounded by the ended fifth seal, Revelation 6:11, and the beginning of the seventh seal. That will be a limited and horrific period; the sixth seal, a World War. Going forward to the end point of the sixth, we come quickly to the seventh seal (third woe); extending onward seven-and-a-half years thru the continued time of *"the vials of the wrath of God"* until Armageddon. That equates to the celebratory, or "victory," supper occupying part, or all, of seven-and-a-half years, and it is on the front end of the Seventh Day. As per the Hebron similitude: David's seven-and-a-half years in Hebron was a definitive part of his Reign. Simply put, the seven thunders, vials, plagues, and wrath of God fall within the first seven-and-a-half years of the millennium reign of Christ.

The seventh chapter, in total, is important because it gives the estate of God's chosen, both terrestrial and celestial. The 144,000 Celestials of the first resurrection are caught up to the throne of God (Revelation 12:5). They are with Christ in rulership and set to witness the wrath of God on the ungodly.

Refreshing the point, while not the focus of this section, verses 4–8 are referring to the first group of 144,000 terrestrial Jews sealed and poised to head the government of God on earth. As to this group, God is now beginning to completely fulfill all the promises made to Abraham; that would be all the promises concerning natural Israel. Many promises relate to the Middle East geography touch the matter of *"Hephzibah, and thy land Beulah: for the Lord delighteth in thee, and thy land shall be married"* (Isaiah 62:4). That qualifies as a "bride message" pertaining to the natural Jew. The people, blessed of God, are married to the land.

Bride of Christ: Election or Other?

Repeating the premise: The message of the Bride is one of the hidden truths of Scripture. The title question asks about the manner, method, and principles integral to gathering the 144,000 of Revelation 14: 1. If the basic premise is hidden, rest assured treating the "formulation" is very "troubling." Thus, the discussion rightfully appears here in the chapter "Troubling Issues."

An important scriptural feature that needs to be restated: The "<u>man child</u> . . . *caught up unto God, and to his throne,"* reappears a thousand years later as *"the <u>bride</u>, the Lamb's wife . . . descending out of heaven from God"* (Revelation 12:5 and 21:9, 10, respectively).

Revelation 14:11 states, *"*<u>Thou</u> *hast created all things, and for* <u>thy</u> *pleasure they are and were created."* The intent of God is: for His pleasure. One aim of this writing is to emphasize that any individual included in the Bride group is as per <u>His pleasure</u>; <u>His choice</u>, not ours. Emphasis on that fact brings predestination into view, and rightfully so. Predestination is a principle vital to the discussion. Romans 8:29 relates to his chosen: be they Jew, the Bride, or other. *"For whom he did foreknow, he also did predestinate to be conformed to the image of his Son."*

It is necessary here that we draw a line between predestination and Calvinism. Calvinism is a viewpoint of predestination that might unfortunately cloud the issue. While predestination is a Bible doctrine, Calvinism is man's explanation or concept of predestination. Regarding that statement: Far be it from us to deny doctrinal correctness or divine inspiration in the matter. Anyone who tries to totally disqualify Calvinism will likely fail. The arguments on this subject run deep and wide. Scholarly minds are committed to its continuance. I do not presume to have the subject in hand. What is mentionable is a root danger. Calvinism must not be perceived as an attempting to define and "qualify" God's omniscience. A wise man does well to humbly "confess" God's omniscience. Again, being more acceptable, we do well in declining entitlement to a prideful approach to the realm of God's omniscience. The safer ground is to "exalt" God's omnipotence. We correctly declare God's limitless power to perform his good will, even in us. Simply put: Bible predestination shows that God's intent <u>is</u>, and that it is <u>irrefutable</u>. It is landscape fraught with pitfalls. That is: A far-reach in Calvinism that might suppose to define and qualify the mindset of God. If so be, that pride is the mother of all sins; pray that any such prideful approach will not get a foothold in the matter.

Faith-believing and embracing the Sovereignty of God concerning the Election is not meant to bring Calvinism into the picture as a sort of proof. Rest assured, God is Sovereign and his predetermined will and plan are going to be brought to pass.

Treating a finer point: pertaining to the "individuality" consideration, that is, concerning the 144,000 in particular. Are those persons more known by "individuality and personality" and not just as being "in Christ," going back to the very time of creation? Wisdom, salted with humility, would caution us against a hard and fast denial on that point. That would be a matter of God's omniscience and unspoken intent. Only the presumptuous would see themselves so privileged; on that point, maybe God only. Jesus made a connected statement in Matthew 20:23, *"To sit on my right hand, and on my left, is not mine to give, but it shall be given to them for whom it is prepared of my father."*

Restating the fact: Our error may be overreaction, even rejecting a principal fact. For example: The term *Sovereignty of God* has become, as some say, a catchword for Calvinism. The great danger in overreaction is that we overturn or discount the fact that <u>God is sovereign</u>. We cannot afford this bending away from the very Nature of our Sovereign God, a truth vital to the pith and marrow of the discussion: "The Plan of God." This tendency becomes an especially dangerous roadblock when related to the truth of the formation of the Bride group or number, 144,000 Celestial (Revelation 14: 1). God forbid that we are guilty of "clouding the issue."

Please note: These statements prove nothing against or for Calvinism. That is not the purpose of this discussion. It serves only to sound a note of caution. If Calvinism does presume too much and overreaches in its grasp, then we must be cautious not to do the same. If you have a fear toward Calvinism, let it not back you away from the position that the High Calling of God is a matter of "election." The "Bride" is the "Spiritual Very Elect." We remain consistent in fearing to exalt to God's chair while judging issues and attempting to explain *"matters, or in things too high for me"* (Psalms 131: 1).

The rejection of God's sovereignty concerning the Bride-selection subject may be the central issue of this writing. If, when we say, "we are striving for the Bride," let it not diminish the fact of God's election of the Bride. We need fear, lest we be found entertaining prideful error. The "Bride," as we term it, is a product of

God's choosing, and that, from a host of overcomers. It is certainly not our sole, personal determination. While we do determine so much, God remains sovereign in this matter of choice. The pitfalls of rejecting this position are many. I will mention eight points worthy of consideration.

First: If the Bride is not by appointment, then it tends to be viewed as a reward of "the race." Thus, emulation may become a problem; at least, as pertains to competitiveness toward our Brother. We think we're in a race to the finish with our Brother. Not so. Paul's statements in Corinthians 9:25–27 *"striveth . . . run . . . fight . . . keep under"* did not refer to any kind of contest with his Brother, nor did *"I press toward the mark for the prize of the high calling of God in Christ Jesus"* (Philippians 3: 14). Paul's, and our, contest or race is against sin and death. The product, or finish, is to be like Jesus. In no sense of the word are we in a competitive race with our brother.

Second: If the High Calling is not by election, then it can be seen as "in our court," not only in the playing court, but also, more importantly, in our court pertaining to judgment, even viewing the reward as proceeding more from our efforts than from God's judgment, love, and grace. Therein lies a dangerous tendency to self-righteousness, even settling for "works." It is easy to give a self-emphasis to the *"hath made herself ready"* (Revelation 19:7). We must read on, *"And to her was* granted *that she should be arrayed in fine linen, clean and white"* (Revelation 19:8). Scripture does state clearly that we do have responsibility in the matter. However, that responsibility, on our part, is to be made conformable, with no tendency to exalt to God's chair.

Third: If we entertain a self-chosen estate, it will lead to a hurtful separation of persons, greater and lesser. We may entertain the idea of prejudicing men and women regarding male over female in bride selection; furthermore, regarding ministry preferred over laity. The basis here is that the self-chosen Bride class, or caste, will be the ministry (celestial), while the laity will likely be something less (terrestrial). While we do believe this is God's plan and that there is a selective rapture of the to-be-celestial chosen, this final placement of any person should not generate a problem. The reason being: We will not hold the issue in our hands. Excellence of spirit and humbleness of mind come only with the confession that the choice is the Lord's. Otherwise, whole churches, as well as individuals, may suppose that they are bride class while relegating others to new earth status. This potential exaltation can be divisive. Shouldn't we humbly rejoice in whatever the Lord decides our eternal life will entail? Paul said, *"God giveth it a body* as it hath pleased him *. . . There are also celestial bodies, and bodies terrestrial: but the glory of the celestial is one, and the glory of the terrestrial is another"* (1 Corinthians 15:38, 40). Note: Again, we make the point: *"as it hath pleased him."* An argument may enter here that the thirty-eighth verse refers to the original creation and does not connect to the fortieth verse. I believe that it exactly connects. Without this understanding imparted in Paul's writing, we would be lacking a necessary point of understanding pertaining to "resurrection," the "bride," and the "rapture." Actually, the message of the bride and a selective rapture is the high-water mark in the doctrine of resurrection. Without this understanding and knowledge of the catching away, the "rapture event" becomes confused and even bizarre.

<u>Fourth</u>: If we discount God as being sovereign in this matter, then we will presume to see ourselves as authors of a sort of greatness. This may lead to aggressive and ambitious conduct to gain people, geography, and power. Close on the heels of this error is a misinterpretation of the parable of the talents and the rewards: Gather and gain station in this life, so I'll have it waiting for me on the other side. Again, even a pride-driven error that would cause us to seek position here that would somehow guarantee a position in the heavenly, may even give rise to behavior contrary to the pathway of charity, which is our true course. *"Charity vaunteth not itself"* (1 Corinthians 13:4).

<u>Fifth</u>: If we seriously deem the Bride class position as self-chosen or self-elect or self-accomplished, then we will negate any genuine heart to *"let each esteem other better than themselves"* (Philippians 2:3). Please note: When we speak of a thing as weighted toward self, that error does not necessarily count God out of the equation. What we are looking at, however, is a slant or bias that will trend to spoil the spirit of this otherwise precious truth. Taken to its end, it could negatively affect our relationship toward one another. We could lose the capacity to be a servant one to another.

<u>Sixth</u>: What about God? How can we truly please him when we are willfully setting ourselves before the heavenly host as one who runs a race against our brother or any other of humanity? How must he perceive us if we <u>presume to set ourselves beside him in the heavens without him having first bid us forward</u>? Also, there is a danger of <u>despising the wonderful New Earth realm as a second and undesirable finish</u>. Please know that this is hurtful in his sight. He loves us still, but this mindset must be forfeited. It lacks thankfulness, humbleness, and meekness.

<u>Seventh</u>: If God chose the twelve, and selects his ministry, then he will surely choose the Bride. Any office, gift, or calling pertaining to an earthly ministry is definitely a lesser station than to be among the celestial 144,000. Reasonably; <u>if</u> the Bride is self-chosen, self-elect, then every office pertaining to this life would be self-chosen. That would discount the fact that God chooses his ministry here among terrestrial mankind.

<u>Eighth</u>: Back to the point of beginning. If the doctrine of Calvinism is assumed to be exalted, in that it presumes to define or even qualify what God desires to know or allow, then is it not likewise exalted for us to deny God his choice and will toward us in the matter of calling?

Concluding thoughts: We need to see the election of the Bride as a sovereign God's sole prerogative. Confessing this, we can realize how that we must strive lawfully for the mastery, and with what spirit. The effort is not toward office or power or self. The desire must be to please God and be pleasant in his sight: *"Holy, harmless, undefiled, separate from sinners"* (Hebrews 7:26). The high calling is as Jesus said, *"To sit on my right hand, and on my left, is not mine to give, but it is shall be given to them for whom it is prepared of my Father"* (Matthew 20:23).

We have a wonderful truth in the message of the Bride. It is very important that we hold this truth in a lawful manner pleasing to God. The spirit of this precious truth is also very important; not just our holding the truth, but holding it lawfully and in the right spirit. Misconception and tradition can alter our perception and slant the message away from the will of its author. In the finality of all things, concerning the total volume of the plan of God, it is said: *"Thou hast created all things, and for thy pleasure they are and were created"* (Revelation 4: 11). The will of its author is *"for thy (God's will) pleasure."*

In all things pertaining to God's Intent, His Word, His Plan: The foundation remains—His pleasure, not ours; His will, not ours; His choice, not ours.

The expression "striving for the Bride" could be a flawed statement. I say "could be" because persons could lack understanding of the first and second considerations pointed out early in this writing. The rejection that is evidenced, when these points are brought to bear, is an indication that understanding is lacking. That evidence would be a reaction that is often in line with the aforementioned eight points. As we grow spiritually, we increasingly know, desire, and yield to His Will. We understand more perfectly that our striving should not be for an office, but to be conformed to the image of His Dear Son, Jesus our Lord. The desire of the righteous is to please him and be favored of him. His desire toward us is that we be overcomers, as per His Ordained Plan. When we speak of the Bride goal in our expression, let it be flavored with the revelation that *"it shall be given to them for whom it is prepared"* (Mark 10:40).

Spirit, Soul, and Body

Following is an abbreviated review on this subject. A more complete treatment appeared earlier in the book. The reason this subject is rehearsed in this "Troubling Issues" chapter is because of the "consequential" misunderstanding of the "spirit" of man as compared to the "soul" of man. It is a blind spot. On that point: We endeavor to rightly divide the word of God. The apostle Paul told Timothy, *"Study to shew thyself approved unto God, a workman that needeth not to be ashamed, rightly dividing the word of truth"* (1 Timothy 2:15).

The teachings and arguments on this subject go back to the time of the early church fathers and forward to the present. If you pursue the subject and spend a few minutes perusing the headlines, you will see that a lifetime of study would not suffice to grasp all that is out there, excuse the expression. That is not our calling. However, I do see some benefit in looking into the teaching presented by others embracing the tripartite nature of man as we see it in Scripture. Our calling and spiritual need is to gain sufficient understanding toward healing a blind spot. This knowledge is a key to understanding the means whereby God heals our spiritual infirmities.

Introducing the basic parameters regarding this subject: There exist two realms, then three; first, the Spirit realm and, second, the material or physical realm. The Spirit realm is God's habitation. As Paul said in Ephesians 4:6, *"One God and Father of all, who is above all, and through all, and in you all."* The material or physical realm was a subsequent second realm brought into existence by the Creator, God. The observable material realm exists within the Spirit realm. God created the plant and animal kingdoms and spoke life into them. More explicitly, God transformed inanimate material into mechanisms that received and perpetuated natural life. That life was not connected to God beyond relating to its natural habitat. After that, he created man. Genesis 2:7 states, *"And the Lord God formed man of the dust of the ground* (body), *and breathed into his nostrils the breath of life* (spirit); *and man became a living soul* (soul)."* To wit: God made the body or tabernacle of a to-be-man. Then, he breathed life, Spirit, into that body and it became a living soul. At that point, Adam was a product and representative of two realms. As such, he was a soul that reflected another third realm, the psychological realm. The psychological, or thought, realm exists within the Spiritual and material/physical realm. God had already created living creatures but they related only to the material natural realm, having no capacity to commune, be led, or have conscience toward God. The animal kingdom being a part of nature was not spiritually connected to God as man was. Again, animals have no God-given communion, conscience, nor intuition, which equates to a spiritually ordained dominion. Animals are alive, but with no thought toward their creator. Animal life and plant life are not God-connected. Man, before the Fall, was God-connected as a spiritual, physical being. After the Fall, man was disconnected spiritually and, having been expelled from the Garden of Eden, he lost communion, conscience, and, more obviously, he lost dominion.

Having known the God connection, and then being void of that, would be the greatest sorrow imaginable. Could it be that when God *"made him to be sin for us, who knew no sin"* (2 Corinthians 5:21), that is; on the cross suffering death in our stead, Jesus felt that separation and cried out, *"My God, my God why has thou forsaken me?"* (Matthew 27:46.) Now, thru the precious saving blood of Jesus Christ, we are reconnected. Romans 8:15, 16, states, *"Ye have received the Spirit of adoption, whereby we cry, Abba, Father. The Spirit itself beareth witness with our spirit, that we are the children of God."* Paul said the same in 1 Corinthians 6:17, *"But he that is joined unto the Lord is one spirit."* The spirit of a born-again person connects to the Spirit realm. God relates to man by the Spirit–spirit connection. *"The Lord weigheth the spirits"* (Proverbs 16:2).

Moving Out a Live Soul (Death and Resurrection Are One Event) vs. Resurrection Teaching (The Person Dies and Resurrects Later)

A more complete discussion on the subject of resurrection appeared earlier. This section treats a particularly difficult and more obscure issue. Foundational in the treatment of death and resurrection are the obvious issues of who, how, when, and where. There are also the difficult and technical questions of conscious or unconscious, clothed upon or naked, and treating related Scriptures as literal versus metaphorical.

We must have truth, with an understanding that the resurrection is not only an event but the estate of Life in God. This estate is referred to by Jesus in Luke 20:36 as *"children of the resurrection."* We prioritize the Life aspect as inherent to resurrection. Lacking that enlightenment, there is a bottomless spiritual void and it is dreadful. It can be termed a "blind spot" in understanding God's plan. Again, resurrection is the estate of Life, and that is, most importantly, a continuing life registered in the Spirit realm. A comparable ownership of a property is yours to have and hold as an in-hand contract; but, at "closing," your papers could be rendered not necessary, in favor of the registered papers of record, which are copied and brought forth and presented by the closer. That is to say, *"Rather rejoice, because your names are written in heaven"* (Luke 10:20). That register is in the Spirit realm, which is "with God." Jesus said, *"Into thy hands* <u>I commend my spirit</u>*: and having said thus, he gave up the ghost"* (Luke 23:46). *"And they stoned Stephen, calling upon God, and saying, Lord Jesus, <u>receive my spirit</u>"* (Acts 7:59). <u>That is the estate of continuing, uninterrupted life.</u> To wit: *"shall never die"* (John 11:26). This is a principal understanding of faith, and is indeed a source of rejoicing. <u>*"For the law of the Spirit of life in Christ Jesus hath made me free from the law of sin and death"*</u> (Romans 8:2).

It is duly noted that Luke and the apostle Paul give the resurrection-related scriptural narrative with added detail, especially differentiating soul and spirit.

The resurrection is to be embraced as Life not death. We are all, I hope, agreed that we move out alive. That is truth and it would be very right to stop there. Unfortunately, we do not rest with this precious estate of Life. We tend to go forward with our additions, including a blind spot as to the differentiation of spirit and soul. The clear "water of life" becomes muddied. Should we not humbly confess to the possibility that our persistence could weary the Lord and his Church? We go forward, wanting to take the "life factor" into our own hands. We want to maintain our consciousness, thinking, will, and emotions; that is, our soul. We are not willing to rest, in the ultimate sense, asleep in God but alive to God. *"for all live unto him"* (Luke 20:38). Help us, Lord, so that by faith we can "give it to God." There must be a "faith factor" in our embrace of resurrection truth. Lacking faith, there is no rest. Lacking faith, Isaiah 28:20 would be a dreadful prospect. To wit: *"Come, my people, enter thou into thy chambers and shut thy doors about thee: hide thyself as it were for a little moment, until the indignation be overpast."* (This Scripture relates specifically to the resurrection of Matthew 27:52, 53, and, forward to the first resurrection, but it reflects a truth and principle concerning the resurrection.) Jesus used the term *"Abraham's bosom"* (Luke 16:22). In typology, Abraham's bosom would be, especially to the Jew, tantamount to the bosom of God; that would be the blessed estate of Life, having passed from living this present life.

The description "moving out a live soul" versus "not moving out a live soul" is an unfortunate misstatement and conflicted in itself. Some blind spots tend to generate division.

Having a healed "blind spot" equates to a corrected perception of spirit, soul, and body. When the spirit of man is quickened by God's power, the spirit in man becomes one with the life of God, who is Spirit. That Holy Ghost operation is God's gift of resurrection. Jesus said, *"And whosoever liveth and believeth in me shall never die. Believest thou this?"* (John 11:26). The answer must be a resounding, "Yes!" That is, we move out alive! Howbeit, not a conscious, active soul, or person, but a live Spirit–spirit. Again, not death but life! Living in God. Assuredly, this knowledge is predicated on an understanding of Spirit, Soul, and Body.

The present teaching of most of mainline religious groups is that, at death, the believer remains alive with continuing consciousness into observance of the third heaven realm. Thus, having immediately gained their celestial estate, they would necessarily have their new bodies. This would be, by definition, the resurrection event, specifically, the first resurrection. More correctly stated, not a resurrection, but a translation from mortal life to immortality, from terrestrial to celestial. Lacking qualification and explanation, it is in error.

On that point, we have heard people laugh about the preacher who puts the dead person in heaven during the service. Later, at the graveside, he speaks of his eventual resurrection. We ought not to laugh. That preacher may not understand every detail of the resurrection doctrine, but his statements may pass as correct, both in the service and graveside. That is, if he, or she, doesn't portray the deceased as acting out his wants and wishes in the heavenly. Correctly stated, if the deceased is heir to a resurrection, being written in the book of life, he does move out alive, *"into Abraham's (God's) bosom,"* and that is a very real phase of resurrection. He moves from conscious mortal life to unconscious, for the most part, and that touches eternal life. Does not the Scripture say, in Christ' discourse with the Sadducees on resurrection, *"all live unto him"* (Luke 20:38). Job 14:14, 15, gives us the correct scenario: *"If a man dies, shall he live again? All the days of my appointed time will I wait, till my change come. Thou shalt call, and I will answer thee: thou wilt have a desire to the work of thine hands."* That call and that answer is that person's resurrection from sleep to a conscious soul.

The teaching against moving out a live soul may seem to be technically correct and scriptural. I have heard it termed, "the resurrection doctrine." But, as taught, it is about "dying," and death is the event. Later, the dead resurrect. The Bible terminology relates it that way: *"The dead."* The understanding that corrects the picture is revealed by Jesus' words. Again, we quote Luke 20:38, *"for all live unto him."* Yes, dead in terms of man's perception, but alive in God; termed *"asleep"* in this narrative.

Only in the instance of those who are alive and remain at his coming for the very elect, 1 Corinthians 15:51, 52, can we see something approaching moving out a live soul. Again, the exception being those that are alive and remain at the time of the "catching away."

In so many words, Jesus revealed the matter: See Mathew 9:23–26 and Luke 8:49–56. Also, see John 11:11–14.

Moving out a live soul is not scripturally provable, but it is, at least, correct in the sense of being flavored with Life. That is important because life exalts over death. That particular point is not a concluding statement and neither is it a trite comment. The answer follows, and it will be both agreeable and disagreeable to both schools of thought.

Refreshing the point: The teacher that takes what seems to be the technically correct scriptural position that the Saints go to the grave as dead, needs to flavor his expressions with the "life aspect." It is a blind spot if we fail to understand that the life of those who are *"children of the resurrection"* are in God and not the deceased. We have "imputed" God life or *"the earnest"* (Ephesians 1:14), and, as pertains to this life, it is our spirit that has been made alive. We are not immortals in ourselves any more than we are righteous in ourselves. Our eternal life is in Him. A deceased child of God is alive in God, and that is in the Spirit realm. Again, see it as alive *"in his bosom"* (Luke 16:23). That is, in the bosom of the Father. Jesus said it plainly, *"Rejoice, because your names are written in heaven"* (Luke 10:20).

A study of spirit and soul will show us that, in certain contexts, what can be said about the spirit can be said about the soul and what can be said about the soul can be said about the spirit. Scriptural usage of those terms, as relates to definition, is per realm and that is contextual. When the Bible uses the term *soul* it may just be referring to the person, with no knowledge or consideration given to the spirit–soul detail, as per Matthew 10:28. Luke 12:5 gives the added detail. If a person, call him a soul, is not born-again of the Spirit and remains disconnected from eternal life, his spirit is not made alive. He is accurately depicted as a soul, or person. They would be as any other creature whose end is to perish.

Refreshing the point: Jesus said, *"Our friend Lazarus sleepeth . . . Then said Jesus unto them plainly, Lazarus is dead"* (John 11:11, 14). Two realms are reflected here. Spirit realm: Lazarus was asleep. Man's earthly, natural, or physical realm: Lazarus was dead. The same insight was demonstrated with the death of the damsel in Matthew 9:24; God's perspective and man's perspective were on display in that instance. When Jesus expressed God's perspective, *"They laughed him to scorn."* It is a blind spot to comprehend the spirit of a Holy Ghost person as only an attitude or disposition. It is where the Life, or Spirit of God, resides and that does not die. As God entertains the spirit of a person, it encompasses the whole person.

It is commonly stated that Jesus died spirit, soul, and body. Scripture does not substantiate that phrase as applied to Jesus or any born-again child of God. To the contrary, in Luke 23:46, Jesus said, at his time of death, *"Father, into thy hands I commend my* <u>spirit</u>: *and having said thus, he gave up the ghost."* Likewise, concerning Stephen at his time of death, *"And they stoned Stephen, calling upon God, and saying, Lord Jesus, receive my* <u>spirit</u>*"* (Acts 7:59). Jesus stated the same to Martha in John 11:26, *"And whosoever liveth and believeth in me shall never die. Believest thou this?"* Jesus, and any person who is heir to a resurrection, could never be spiritually dead. Being spiritually dead is a state, or condition, suiting the unsaved or those who were once saved and then later were lost. That qualifies as *"twice dead"* (Jude 12). The state of the saved, being heirs to a resurrection, is Life. Jesus said that, *"For he is not a God of the dead, but of the living:* <u>for all live unto him</u>*"* (Luke 20:38). Paul states, *"Whether we live therefore, or die, we are the Lord's"* (Romans 14:8).

The corrected expression is *move out a live spirit.* Afterward, as Paul stated in 1 Corinthians 15:38, *"God giveth it a body as it hath pleased him, and to every seed his own body."* It is possible we are coming to the place in God, as provided by our Lord Jesus Christ, that we not only give up our rights regarding fleshly living, but making the next step, and, by faith, give up our own living, and then, having that hope, rest in the hands of God, in Jesus Christ. Help us, Lord, so that by faith we can "give it to God."

Restoration of the Jew or Replacement Theology?

There is a current and growing belief that that the Jewish people will lose their "chosen" status and be replaced by the Church. This persuasion has the effect of moving a Christian to the rank of opposing God's intent for the Jewish people. That dread may be on our schedule of things coming. The spiritual offence is presuming to erase a promise God made to his people, a promise that is not going to be overturned or marginalized. That will not happen. You can expect to see a rising tide of anger, contention, and malice on this point. The purview of how the Plan of God will progress for the Jew was given earlier in the book, within the discussion on resurrection; especially, the section dealing with Revelation 7.

The promises made to Abraham pertained to the geography and control of the land. A people "married to the land." Coincidently, that geography of Jerusalem, and the surrounding territory, will be the location from which the Lord rules. It will be the landing place for the *"holy Jerusalem, descending out of heaven from God"* (Revelation 21:10). That is a spiritual *"great city,"* but it integrates wonderfully and complementary with the natural city of Jerusalem. It is that glorious union of the two "bride" messages: The celestial 144,000 married to Christ and the 144,000 terrestrial Jews blessedly married to the land. This narrative in the twenty-first chapter of Revelation is the concluding glory that began one thousand years earlier with the 144,000 Jewish leadership *"sealed"* and the 144,000 *"man child"* being *"caught up unto God"* (Revelation 7:4 and 12:5, respectively).

As the Plan progresses, the remnants of the Church, Jew and Gentile, are wonderfully integrated, seamless, going into Christ's millennial reign. It is the initiation of a new heaven and a new earth. Perish the worry that somehow the non-Jew will be a second-class citizen, *"For ye are all the children of God by faith in Christ Jesus. For as many of you as have been baptized into Christ have put on Christ. There is neither Jew nor Greek, there is neither bond nor free, there is neither male nor female: for ye are all one in Christ Jesus. And if ye be Christ's, then are ye Abraham's seed, and heirs according to the promise"* (Galatians 3:26–29).

Organization

Attributing every doctrine and precept taught by the founding fathers as a landmark and irrefutable is an easy and accommodating place of rest. Contrariwise, waiting on the dispensation of greater authority and truth, at the time of the Lord's choosing, is sometimes God's more perfect will.

Embracing the original foundation of a movement is almost always the path to acceptance and promotion. In the matter of origins of the movement, declaring every teaching of the founding fathers as irrefutable and attaching that status to themselves is exalting. It hinders furthering the revelation of God's plan. Alternatively, a totally unproductive liberal exaltation would be to scrap the past and move on. These disparities are the prime ingredients for "stop here" or otherwise "a split." There is a ditch on both sides of the High Way. The pathway or High Way of Charity, in its pure form, is priceless. Because Christians love God, and because they love others, they are survivors, separated from worldliness, and hoping to be spared the pitfall of *organization*, whose synonym is often "division."

We witness great zeal in holding fast to a past teaching as a matter of loyalty to a precept we think of as foundational. Reasonably, this kind of adherence may be used as validation or personal exaltation, especially if it is attached to the fact of tenure and ability. Name-dropping is a close-kin tactic. There is that possibility that adherents of some doctrine are intransigent, when the originator would have yielded to a more correct and applicable present truth. On that point, we do know that past leadership, if they were on station now, would embrace going forward and changing for the benefit of a more spiritual, complete, and accurate understanding. This kind of entrenchment is possibly the most truth limiting and destructive earmark of organization. When doctrinal disputes arise, godly men <u>avoid</u> positioning themselves as infallible; or even the idea that their perspective and knowledge will exhaust the subject. They would reject such a position and so would any reasonable participant. We should not attribute such a fearful stance to certain of our forefathers, when, in actuality, they would regard infallibility as fitting only the Lord Jesus, the Apostles, and Scripture. In a sense, let us not reproach the dead.

In 1 Corinthians 15:53, it states: *"For this corruptible must put on incorruption, and this mortal must put on immortality."* It is an overreach to claim that estate before the time. Please understand that a similar and related overreach would be to claim infallibility relating to doctrine. Infallibility is the highest chair and has the potential of doing the greatest good. If such a claim is a case of mistaken identity, it will hurt the Church. If the claim is bogus and intentioned to overreach, then the spirit is afflicted as well as the understanding, so that even greater damage is done. Instead of God's plan and intentions being declared, the individual turns that vision off and lights up his own persona. That would be akin to Isaiah 50:11, *"Walk in the light of your fire, and in the sparks that ye have kindled."*

Remember Jesus' words; *"Enter ye in at the strait gate: for wide is the gate, and broad is the way, that leadeth to destruction, and many there be which go in thereat"* (Matthew 7:13). It is God, not you, who moves the mountain, and that is if he elects to do the thing. God, thru Christ, has elected many times to move the mountains in your individual life. This we surely know. Organizational ties are not easily broken. Noteworthy is the authentic love we have for "our own," to wit: the organization.

Serious consideration is in order. Knowing the Plan of God requires proper footing. We are looking at a primary determination of our perception of God. Your prospect of eternal life depends on how you entertain the love and grace of God. A present-day danger for Pastors and Teachers is that they fail to put their adherents "in Christ," but rather in organized orders and creeds and tradition. That is not a good place to be, especially if conformity renders your eternal life at risk. I find that change is difficult and costly and that conduct is easier said than done.

We are within our God given rights to check out the origins, people involved, and the politics of any pursuit. Look carefully at their ladders of ascendency. Look up to the top rung. In such a case, if Jesus is not the head of the body, then it is not the body of Christ. Worst case scenario: The higher you go the more secular and political. That is the prerequisite for a marriage of civil–religious, which defines false religion; the nefarious aspect of the Plan and that part which *"passeth away"* (1 John 2:17).

The End-Time Message

It is hoped that the reader does, or will, entertain an end-time message. Please understand that "dispensationalism" is not embraced by all religious entities. The root of our dispensationalism is; "God does provide."

John states, *"He gave (dispensed) his only begotton Son,"* and he will give (dispense) righteous judgment toward the *"restitution of all things."* The treatment of that fact is beyond discussion at this juncture of the book. The several schools of thought having to do with prophecies, past or future, carry with them more than can be given in summary. We proceed forward in the narrative accepting that God dispenses helps from heaven at predetermined times. The seventh day will be preceded by the ending of Gentile times, and that with an extraordinary series of judgments. Those judgments, which include great revelation of God's power and determination, along with the entry into the seventh one-thousand-year day, constitute the time frame of an end-time message. This is an important discussion relating to the "Plan of God," and it speaks to "our part" in the Plan for the Body of Christ. The Ecclesia.

We are approaching the end of an age. Religious bodies are seriously fragmented. As an imperative, many organizations will, and have, come together on the basis of laws and precepts with their faith in secular agreements and oversight. The children of God desire a coming together on better basis. The basis being, Christ is the head of the Body. The call will be to partner with God's plan, and with the Lord in a "coming together." That call is necessarily commensurate with another call to un-agenda, which is *"another voice from heaven, saying, Come out of her, my people, that ye be not partakers of her sins, and that ye receive not of her plagues"* (Revelation 18:4). Righteous government is not "structure," it is "God-ordained officiation."

This query of "end-time things" connects well with the next item. To wit:

Pre-, Mid-, or Post-Tribulation Rapture?

The controversy of timing for the rapture, or catching away, troubles our unity on that front. A brief discussion of the correct basic parameters may serve to defuse the contest.

As far as the word *tribulation*, it is consistently *"thlipsis"* in the Greek. It can be literal or figurative, but it doesn't have hidden inuendo attached. As per Strong's Concordance, it is just what we think it means: "pressure, affliction, persecution, anguish, and trouble." Regardless of the source of the Tribulation, it is the correct terminology.

Any reasonable person prefers to avoid pain and suffering. A loving God delights to save and spare his children. Qualifier: That is true excepting times when persecution adds to the perfecting of his Saints and when their suffering and martyrdom serves to complete, *"finished,"* the Plan. After all, Jesus' suffering death *"finished,"* or concluded, the judgment of all things at that happening. The pre-Tribulation rapture does see the church, at least the very elect, leaving before the scene of "greater trouble" arises. Agreed. The "greater trouble" is when the whole of the matter moves from the "wrath of man and demon" to the "wrath of God." Most vital, in the correct treatment of the event of the rapture, is to understand from what <u>source</u> and to whom is the wrath directed. The sequence of event was shown earlier in the subheading "Charts," pages 97 and 101. Beyond those helps, we'll talk it thru:

The last hour begins when *"ten kings, which have received no kingdom as yet; but receive power as kings one hour with the beast . . . and shall give their power and strength unto the beast."* In the same time frame, the Gentiles, a world force, begins occupation of Jerusalem *"and the holy city shall they tread under foot forty and two months"* (Revelation 17:12, 13, and 11:2, respectively. Those markers begin the first forty-two months, or three-and-a-half years, of the last hour. (The time is related in months because it relates to the Jews, which relate to the Law and the state of the Jew at that immediate time; the "moon" is the principal. When days or years are given it relates to the "sun," and that similitude refers to the Church and the dispensation of Christ's sacrifice.)

This first three-and-a-half-year period includes persecution of the Church and the Church prevails for three-and-a-half years. *"The gates of hell shall not prevail against it"* (Matthew 16:18). Relating to the subject's title question: This period does equate to great tribulation and suffering at the hands of the religious–secular powers. Scripture announces that the Tribulation awaits the Church. It is part of the perfection of the Saints' collective, which is the Church. The important fact here is that this tribulation arises from powers contrary to God and the resulting suffering of the Saints is unto the glory of God. It gives forth justification of His coming righteous judgments.

The next three-and-a-half years sees the introduction of demonic forces. It is the defining feature of the transition from the seventh beast to the eighth beast. It happens when *"they shall have finished their testimony."* Furthermore, *"The beast that ascendeth out of the bottomless pit shall make war against them, and shall overcome them, and kill them"* (Revelation 11:7). The two witnesses are *"archon"* or head angels described further as *"olive trees"* and *"candlesticks standing before the God of the earth"* (Revelation 11:3, 4). They are the heavenly component and they integrate Spirit–spirit with the perfected terrestrial martyrs on earth.

This second-mention time of three-and-a-half years is a God-in-observance and God-allowed martyrdom of the remaining very elect, and others. Heaven and earth is judged and the catching away has come. The seventh-day millennium-reign begins with seven-and-a-half years of seven vials' wrath of God leading up to Armageddon. You may reasonably raise the question: Doesn't this put Armageddon seven-and-a-half years into the millennium? Yes, it does. The similitude brought to bear is that David reigned seven-and-a-half years in Hebron before he took Jerusalem. Hebron is a type of heaven, in this instance, where Isaac took Rebecca into his mother's tent. This seven-and-a-half years is that time in heaven from the rapture till Jerusalem is taken. Armageddon is the event. This seven-and-a-half years in Hebron was attributed to David's reign and that similitude indicates that the first seven-and-a-half years immediately after the "catching away" is part of the one-thousand-year reign of Christ. The similitude is fitting, both time and place.

A more concise answer to the title question: The believer will experience the wrath of man and demon. Many will die a martyr's death and that to the glory of God. Those who live thru that three-and-a-half year of persecution and the second three-and-a-half-year time of martyrdom will be protected by friends, and the host of heaven, toward their integration with the initiation of the Jerusalem headquartered kingdom of God on earth. <u>What is most important is that we will not be on the receiving end of the wrath of God</u>. Scripture teaches a "pre-Tribulation rapture," <u>if</u> the "Tribulation" equates to the "wrath of God."

Hopefully, the above explanation will tend to "defuse the issue." Repeating: A pre-Tribulation rapture is right, if the Tribulation is understood to be that time of outpouring of God's wrath. This does not disallow suffering and persecution of believers at the hands of contrary human and demonic spirits. Also, the ones raptured are the many thousands of the "man child," or later termed "bride," who are the remnant of the total 144,000. That would be a very small comparison to the multitude of believers. The overriding Good News is that the multitude of "left-behind believers" are sanctified, covered by the blood of Christ, and spared the impending wrath of God.

The Soul: Mortal or Immortal?

A primary concern that attends this article is the possibility that the reader will outrightly reject any discussion touching a subject so generally embraced as that the soul is immortal. Belief that the soul of every person is immortal is set forth as integral to one's statement of faith. It is a "determinate" as to a person's or group's legitimacy or worth of consideration.

Hand in glove is the treatment of the burning hell doctrine that is firmly held by most Christians. Any variation will predictably elicit a verdict of being non-Christian. Rest assured, there is no wiggle room on this subject. After all, if there is no hell, then there is no heaven.

The doctrines of <u>eternal judgment</u>, and the <u>immortality of the soul</u> are the two-tiered foundation of mainline religious thought explaining the hereafter. "Tradition" is the primary preservative that retards any spoiling of this "main stay."

It is a <u>fact</u> that God is eternal and his concluding judgments are immutable and unending. Add that fact to the <u>premise</u> that all souls are immortal and you have the principal ingredients needed for an unbelievably horrific eternity, reserved and ongoing, for the damned. Those who question the latter premise, that the soul is immortal, would be courting this most-accepted doctrine as a half-truth. Lacking the "threatening" aspect of "hell," the force of the message is rendered lame. There is a heaven to be gained and a hell to be shunned. This real fear often moves the sinner to repent and initiate good actions toward the kingdom of God. As a "tradition," the whole matter is rock solid.

Going beyond tradition, while no one should deny a scriptural hell, it is reasonable to ask, is the subject meant to be cast in bronze? Do we have this aspect of the "plan" accurately and completely portrayed? We might not exercise the liberty to challenge what God, via Scripture, says about a doctrine, but he does ordain that we search for truth. Aside from tradition, what does Scripture say about the matter?

Where the big hole appears is that Scripture is plain in its portrayal of the soul as mortal, and that cannot be gotten around. Another fact that cannot be ignored is the magnitude of error that is implicit in a wrong treatment of this doctrine. Studious minds have guesstimated the totality of humans born, up to this point in history, to approximate 100 billion. Most fundamentalist thinkers would estimate the damned to be +99 billion. The natural mind is not sufficiently endowed to comprehend the magnitude of such an enormous and eternal horror. If it's a lie on God, it's big. Reasonable thinkers will cast this viewpoint on "hell" into the rank of the "bizarre." While God is not beholding to our "reasonable thinking," he is just and our thinking is fundamentally God-given. Think it not strange that a fully indoctrinated and compliant individual would ponder the implications.

Misstatements about God may be mankind's most reoccurring foible, and our Lord doesn't seem moved by that. Moving forward, expect contest and disparity to arise as we go from "Religiosity to Theology." That would be transitioning from knowing and acquiescing to the creeds and settlements of fallible men, to knowing the True God. *Knowing* is used here with the implication of "conception," and to be pregnant with an accepted mindset is not easily undone.

Error in the "spirit" of this most critical matter would be that part which would more likely try God's patience. On our part, such an error might be a "marker" of a spiritual sort; in which case, we need to open our minds and hearts for the most difficult corrections. Acceptance of this indoctrination will mightily flavor your perception of the "spirit" of God's plan.

In the greater landscape, it may be flavoring the whole of societal judgments as they see Christianity. Beyond believers, Christian philosophy spills into every segment of society. I know of no such "societal impact study" having been done or reported. That specific "not knowing," does not disallow the opinion that the overwhelming majority of unbelieving folks see our God as cruel and vindictive.

Short of God imparting immortality, man remains a mortal. Again, the question: Is it likely that cursed-to-die humanity, by procreation, can produce immortals? A thoughtful pause on that point is in order. If the more correct answer is no, then God would necessarily, by imputing immortality, go beyond the human lifespan of torment, onto eternal, never ending horror, to accomplish "hell" as taught. However despised, some will see "annihilationism" as a more fitting doctrinal recourse.

However you review the premises, you will experience rejection. Maybe, even self-rejection. Maybe, even self-loathing. That reality moves people to forget, even discount, the *"harmless"* feature that is Christlike, by extension, Godlike.

We believe the devil *"is a liar, and the father of it"* (John 8:44). He fathered that "mistaken identity." *"Ye shall not surely die"* (Genesis 3:4). Possibly, Eve entertained immortality and mistook her eternal life as immortality. Whichever, she lost her eternal life. She was terrestrial and not an immortal being. The lie was a deception. Eve confessed: *"The serpent beguiled me, and I did eat"* (Genesis 3:13).

The prospect that this troubling doctrinal subject has landed on the enemy's runway and, furthermore, hangared this doctrinal "settlement" there, is ominous, putting it mildly.

The philosophical teachings of Jesus' day were both influential and persuasive, and lent themselves to cloaking the truth. And, Jesus did hide the truth. To wit: Matthew 13:11–15. *"He answered and said unto them,*

Because it is given unto you to know the mysteries of the kingdom of heaven, but to them it is not given. For whosoever hath, to him shall be given, and he shall have more abundance: but whosoever hath not, from him shall be taken away even that he hath. Therefore speak I to them in parables: because they seeing see not; and hearing they hear not, neither do they understand. And in them is fulfilled the prophecy of Isaiah, which saith, By hearing ye shall hear, and shall not understand; and seeing ye shall see, and shall not perceive: For this people's heart is waxed gross, and their ears are dull of hearing, and their eyes they have closed; lest at any time they should see with their eyes, and hear with their ears, and should understand with their heart, and should be converted, and I should heal them."

Jesus spoke of deception, *"And if the blind lead the blind, both shall fall into the ditch"* (Matthew 15:14).

God's judgments are given as eternal, and they are. The similitudes are related to the hearers as if life-perpetuating for that same reason; God is eternal. His fire is eternal because no one can quench his fire; it consumes utterly. The smoke from his fire ascends up for ever and ever because his judgment cannot be altered. A person, within himself, is not eternal. Again, only by God's provision is the individual imparted immortality or eternal life. *"To them who by patient continuance in well doing seek for glory and honour and immortality, eternal life"* (Romans 2:7). Only thus is man going to live on, and God does the imparting. Since the text puts this imparting as a favorable judgment, the reader may be given to further pause.

God is a good God and His Plan is altogether lovely. We, as pastors and teachers, correctly give emphasis to the dreadful estate of an eternal separation from our wonderful God.

The Godhead
Touching the Popular Embrace of Traditional Doctrine and Accepted Creeds

Long-standing historical settlements of doctrines "occupy" with the expectation of compliance, even loyalty toward those orders determined by those creeds. There is little wiggle room for additions or change. Added insights to established teaching puts an expositor on thin ice. Simply put: slight to no consideration for increased understanding, even in the face of needed illumination in this end of the age. The primary concern relating to this subject is that the required subscription to traditional doctrine sets forth a sort of litmus test as to a person's or group's legitimacy. Any straying from doctrine strongly held by the majority may elicit a verdict of being non-Christian. While many Christians admit to the difficulty explaining the Godhead and nomenclature peculiar to its teachings, the "mindset" is staunchly held. An overriding concern is that needed clarification toward remedies would discourage accepting Christians.

Settlements on the subject have roots in the arguments and agreements of the early synods. Going forward, the proponents of presently accepted theology and foundational Protestant doctrine are learned theologians. Notwithstanding, these expositors, excepting papal status, do not claim that their perception, understanding, and portrayal of Scripture is blessed with infallibility. Their imputing of infallibility, if so be, seems to hark back to the originators of said creeds. Whatever that ramification, this doctrine's status in "staid creedal religion" constitutes a coercion to line up, even an encirclement that will help advance a further move toward ecumenism. Any breech can beget fears of rejection and move people to discount the *"harmless"* feature that is Christlike, even sacrificing a more perfect present truth. Recognizing that prospect, it would be wise to consider lest we violate a Godly principle: *"Take heed to your spirit . . . he (God) hateth putting away"* (Malachi 2:15, 16). Anything less than an *"enlarged heart"* constitutes a cessation of gathering the greater truth. No Ecclesia should be burdened with the lack of, or discounting of, greater truth. Void of added truth, we are guaranteed ongoing divisions and eventually spiritual entrenchment, and that is not of God. That is not His Plan for his children.

The first statement and the starting point of the Godhead confession is that Jesus was not merely a figure of history. He is eternal and is, always and forever, the Son of God. He was God's manifestation in the flesh and he is glorified to immortal and celestial, and he is Divinity. Furthermore, Jesus is the one and only "door" of reconciliation with God. He is the one and only predestined and finished at-one-ment, dispensed from heaven and returned to heaven. He alone is our atonement.

We cannot exhaust the expression of God's magnitude, nor can we fully entertain the greatness of the Father, the Son, and the Holy Ghost. However spiritual the person, still, *"now we see through a glass, darkly."*

The greatness of the Head God declares that his "plan for humanity" is great. In that light, let us consider Acts 10:38, *"How God anointed Jesus of Nazareth with the Holy Ghost and with power."*

The apostle Peter is stating that God is the anoint<u>er</u> and Jesus is the anoint<u>ed</u> and the Holy Ghost is the anoint<u>ing</u> (faciliatory).

Relating to this Scripture, and speaking of the Holy Ghost expressly, the apostle Paul related to the Colossians, 1:27, that it was a *"mystery . . . which is* <u>Christ in you</u>, *the hope of glory."* That equates to "son ship." That equates to "family of God." Hebrews 3:6 states, *"Christ as a son over his own house; whose house are we, if we hold fast the confidence and the rejoicing of the hope firm unto the end."* Jesus stated the original premises in John 14:2, *"In my father's house (household) are many mansions: if it were not so, I would have told you. I go to prepare a place for you."* The Holy Spirit facilitates the path to overcoming unto perfection and sonship.

Continuing with the thought of "Christ in you," Jesus said, *"The Spirit of truth; whom the world cannot receive, because it seeth him not, neither knoweth him: but ye know him; for he dwelleth with you, and shall be* <u>in you</u>*"* (John 14:17); the same as the *"Comforter,"* and the *"Spirit of truth"* (John 16:7, 13). The "in you" happened on the Day of Pentecost.

You are encouraged and you are able to reference several Scriptures that convey these thoughts. Also, refresh the Holy Ghost facilitating of Love, Leading, and Learning, et cetera, per "God's Will and Means" (chapter IV).

It is correct to treat the Holy Ghost as a person <u>if</u> we understand and can qualify that person as *"Christ in you."* Think it not strange that God's plan is inclusive, so that we would be integral and primary as the product of the facilitator, which is the Holy Ghost. Call it a Grace ordered "graduation to family." In terms of "order,"

1 Corinthians 11:3 states it thus: *"The head of every* <u>man</u> *is Christ; and the head of the woman is the man; and the head of* <u>Christ</u> *is* <u>God</u>. *"* The rendering: God – Christ – man. Best termed: God – Christ – Holy Spirit, born-again man. Looking to the fullness of the operation, Revelation 3:21 says, *"To him that overcometh will I grant to sit with me in my throne, even as I also overcame, and am set down with my Father in his throne."*

Again, the "Plan" is great because the Author is great. As has been stated earlier, a restored and "finished" mankind is at the forefront of the "Plan." Back to the basic premise: This is about "family."

The total and absolute knowledge of the Godhead touches infinity, and it cannot humanly be exhausted. To think otherwise would be a blind spot. So be it, if God allows, and if the end time requires, there will be more revelation of the Creator's Plan, even more detail of his intent and Godhead. Addressing the theological landscape, it bears repeating, this writing will not move the peg. Pray that God allows greater light, issued from greater powers, for the sake of the Body of Christ.

Reviewing the "Greater Landscape"

Your embrace of godliness is flavored by how you entertain the majesty and divinity of our Lord and Savior Jesus Christ. Conformity to an agreed to cessation of growing in knowledge, as per a cast-in-bronze settlement, may limit your spiritual growth. To wit: *"And Jesus* <u>increased</u> *in wisdom and stature, and in favor with God and man"* (Luke 2:52). In the church scenario: *"*<u>increaseth</u> *with the increase of God"* (Colossians 2:19). Don't sacrifice the more perfect knowledge of God's intent and plan in favor of perpetuating your "comfort zone."

The majority of folks rest doctrinal settlements on the principals laid down by learned men of old; disciplined and principled men, schooled in <u>their</u> "present truth." That history is beyond this short and abbreviated article. Without contest, we see presently embraced mainline doctrine as "settlements" arrived at in the historical arena of contesting both heresies and truth.

Jesus is eternal inasmuch as he proceeded from the Eternal Father. *"In the beginning was the Word, and the Word was* <u>with God</u>*, and the Word* <u>was God</u>*"* (John 1:1). Read on, verse 14: *"And the Word was made flesh, and dwelt among us (and we beheld his glory, the glory as of the only begotten of the Father), full of grace and truth."* Later, in 17:5, *"And now, O Father, glorify thou me with thine own self with the glory which I had* <u>with thee</u> *before the world was."*

How is it that Jesus *"was God"* and, simultaneously, *"with"* the Father? Answer: Simply because *"God . . . calleth those things which be not as though they were"* (Romans 4:17). Integrate that thought with the fact that *"Word,"* logos, in John 1:1, has the meaning of intent or plan and we see that <u>Jesus is eternally, the Plan and Intent of Eternal God</u>. Jesus, proceeding from, or coming forth from Eternal God equates to being eternal with God. Jesus is the A to Z of God's creation. As per Jesus justifying the continuance of all things, he is the basis for the *"restitution of all things."* Lacking faith and a spirit of confession, such a concept is beyond our grasp. This is not a play on words or mind game. Without Christ's advent and him fulfilling all things, everything goes away. Why wouldn't he be the Heir and counted the *"by him, and for him"* of Colossians 1:16? Allowing for clarification and qualifying the statement, we could say that Jesus the Son, in an ethereal reality, was a unity with God the Father before *"the Word was made flesh"* and after *"the Word was made flesh"* in a literal, manifest sense.

Regarding predeterminations: If there is any exaltation in expressing our knowledge, let it be in the realm of God's omni<u>potence</u>. Approaching or qualifying God's omni<u>science</u> is beyond our capabilities. In 1 Timothy 6:16, speaking of God's omniscience, it states: *"Who only hath immortality, dwelling in <u>the light</u> which <u>no man can approach unto</u>; <u>whom no man hath seen, nor can see</u>: to whom be honour and power everlasting. Amen."* A better resting place is to <u>confess the reality of his omniscience</u> and, going forward, <u>speak declarative of his omnipotence</u>.

We cannot limit God, as if he could not entertain the pre-virgin birth Christ, and delight to see his *"wisdom"* revealed when the *"Word"* would be *"made flesh."* The fact is plainly stated. *"The Lord possessed me in the beginning of his way, before his works of old. I was set up from everlasting, from the beginning, or ever the earth was. When there were no depths, I was brought forth; when there were no fountains abounding with water. Before the mountains were settled, before the hills was I brought forth: While as yet he had not made the earth, nor the fields, nor the highest part of the dust of the world, when he prepared the heavens, I was there: when he set a compass upon the face of the depth: When he established the clouds above: when he strengthened the fountains of the deep: When he gave to the sea his decree, that the waters should not pass his commandment: when he appointed the foundations of the earth: Then I was by him, as one brought up with him: and I was daily his delight, rejoicing always before him"* (Proverbs 8:22–30). These verses speak to the wisdom of God, the same as the predetermined Christ, and no less an 'individuality.' That is, *"with God"* before the advent of Jesus of Nazareth, then, after his birth, into *"a body hast thou prepared me"* (Hebrews 10:5). The apostle Paul addresses this understanding in Ephesians 3:8–11. *"Unto me, who am less than the least of all saints, is this grace given, that I should preach among the Gentiles the unsearchable riches of Christ; And to make all men see what is the fellowship of the <u>mystery</u>, which from the beginning of the world hath been <u>hid in God</u>, who created all things by Jesus Christ: To the intent that now unto the principalities and powers in heavenly places might be known by the church the manifold wisdom of God, According to the eternal purpose which he purposed in Christ Jesus our Lord."*

We may be confined within time and dimension, but God has no confinements or limitations whatsoever. That realization, flavored with humility, is foundational to this understanding.

There is no exclusivity when it comes to understanding and experiencing sonship with Christ; exalting and loving the one and only God and his dear Son. The conversion that allows right perspective and conduct is to know the *"One God and Father of all, who is above all, and through all, and in you all"* (Ephesians 4:6). When Jesus is truly in our heart, there should be a shared love and not a spirit of putting away. That is the estate of a Holy Ghost child of God, *"which is Christ in you, the hope of glory"* (Colossians 1:27). This *"glory"* is the same *"glory"* mentioned in John 17:5, *"And now O Father, glorify thou me with thine own self with the glory which I had with thee before the world was."* This understanding is bedrock to our affinity to God's plan. Again, it is the deeper reality of Christ-in-us, *"This mystery . . . which is Christ in you, the hope of glory"* (Colossians 1:27).

Jesus is the very heartbeat of God pertaining to the whole matter of creation and the redemption of a flawed world. How great is our Lord? John the Beloved had it right. The Logos or Plan and Intent of God, as he correctly expressed it in John, reference a divine individuality. He knew and stated the Word, Logos, as a reality. The same John the Revelator received and recorded the same, *"Saying, I am Alpha and Omega, the first and the last"* (Revelation 1:11). Please understand, by revelation or confession, that Jesus was with the Father even before his advent of being personified in flesh and blood. Embrace the *"Word"* as an individuality: the precious and eternal son of God and our Lord Jesus Christ. History declares that he was "Son of man" and is "Son of God." Substantively, "like God" and glorified to "same as God." Jesus was glorified on the mountain, in the presence of Moses and Elijah, and he was glorified pre-Ascension in the presence of his awestruck disciples. Allowing fitting historical portrayals, Jesus is eternal Divinity and eternal Perfect Man.

Paul's exhortation in 1 Corinthians 2:5–8: *"That your faith should not stand in the wisdom of men, but in the power of God. Howbeit we speak wisdom among them that are perfect: yet not the wisdom of this world, nor of the princes of this world, that come to nought: But we speak the wisdom of God in a mystery, even the hidden wisdom, which God ordained before the world unto out glory: Which none of the princes of this world knew: for had they known it, they would not have crucified the Lord of glory."* Again, Ephesians 3:9: *"And to make all men see what is the fellowship of the mystery, which from the beginning of the world hath been hid in God, who created all things by Jesus Christ."*

Pertaining to Christ's advent as Son-of-man-terrestrial in the flesh, being also the Son of God, and then subsequently graduating to Son-of-God-celestial:

"Concerning his Son Jesus Christ our Lord, which was made of <u>seed of David according to the flesh</u>*; And declared to be the* <u>Son of God with power, according to the spirit of holiness, by the resurrection from the dead"</u> (Romans 1:3, 4).

Pertaining to the fullness of Christ's reign as King of Kings: *"Then cometh the end, when he shall have delivered up the kingdom to God, even the Father; when he shall have put down all rule and all authority and power. For he must reign, till he hath put all enemies under his feet. The last enemy that shall be destroyed is death. For he hath put all things under his feet.* <u>But when he saith all things are put under him (Jesus Christ), it is manifest that he (Father God) is excepted, which did put all things under him (Jesus Christ).</u> *And when all things shall be subdued unto him* (Jesus Christ), <u>then shall the Son also himself (Jesus Christ) be subject unto him (Father God) that put all things under him (Jesus Christ), that God (Father God) may be all in all"</u> (1 Corinthians 15:24–28).

When our understanding requires, and a God-ordained mandate so requires, then, *"Let us go forth therefore unto him without the camp, bearing his reproach"* (Hebrews 13:13). That is, without the camp of strict traditional demands. Give consideration for clarifications and a more "fullness" of understanding? A tall order? Yes, but it may be your calling. Embrace the dynamic of progressing in the example of our precious Lord. Jesus said, Matthew 16:18, *"Upon this rock I will build my church; and the gates of hell shall not prevail against it."* The church is dynamic. Contrawise, it is the gates of hell that are static. Again; *"And the Word was made flesh, and dwelt among us (and we beheld his glory, the glory as of the only begotten of the Father), full of grace and truth"* (John 1:14).

A seconding of our expression of encouragement toward this *"thing"* and the whole *"matter"* (Proverbs 25:2), *"It is the glory of God to conceal a thing: but the honour of kings is to search out a matter."*

Love, Judgment, Jacob's Ladder, and the 1,600 Furlongs of Revelation 14:20

THE FOUR ITEMS OF the title integrate as the article progresses. Love is foundational and uppermost. Love is preeminent. All things pertaining to God's plan begin with *"For God so loved the world, that he gave his only begotten Son"* (John 3:16). Think of it as the road we travel; call it "the pathway of charity." The called-of-God are traveling West. To wit: That expression reflects our entry and progress in the plan of eternal life. The salvation plan is depicted by the Tabernacle in the Wilderness. Enter on the East side and progress Westward; Courts–Holy Place–Holiest Place. Any other path or direction is eternal death and destruction.

God so loves his creatures and creation that he has determined to eternally sustain that which does not offend, and destroy eternally all that does offend. That fundamental precept reveals God's love as being the heartbeat of the doctrine of eternal judgment. Jesus is the Rock upon which it rests. Jesus is the *"Alpha and Omega"* of God's plan. To wit:

Love: Again, for emphasis, *"For God so loved the world, that he gave his only begotten Son, that whosoever believeth in him should not perish, but have everlasting life"* (John 3:16). This often-quoted Scripture addresses God's love and the prospect of judgment unto eternal life as opposed to eternal death: to perish. Rest assured, God's *"Word"*/ logos, *"intent"*/plan, was Jesus, and in God's realm of creativity it was essentially God himself, later personified in flesh. *"And the Word was made flesh, and dwelt among us"* (John 1:14). Jesus proceeded from God, having been with God as God. *"And now, O Father, glorify thou me with thine own self with the glory which I had with thee before the world was"* (John 17:5).

God ordains all that continues into eternity, and only those "in Christ" have that continuing estate. He loves his creation and being Father and Creator, we can be certain that his will is going to prevail. His love for the creation, especially that part which is his image, ensures that sin in the heavens (spirit realm) and sin in the earth (material realm) will be destroyed eternally.

Ministers of God preach, with conviction and with zeal, that all iniquity shall be overturned entirely. In the spirit of Elisha, we are to comply till God's will prevails and evil be overtaken. There must be no lack of godly fervor, as King Joash lacked in the instance of 2 Kings 13:18, 19. *"He (Elisha) said unto the king of Israel, Smite upon the ground. And he smote thrice, and stayed. And the man of God was wroth with him, and said, Thou shouldest have smitten five or six times."* Ministering God's plan will demonstrate a commitment to doing his will toward overturning, overturning, overturning, overturning, overturning, overturning, first heaven and first earth! Essentially, it is our vision and the message of the Bride; the message of *"The kingdom of heaven is at hand"* (Matthew 10:7).

God's <u>love</u> is the cause, basis, and mandate toward <u>eternal judgment</u>, which equates to total restoration. The apostle Paul, in 1 Timothy 1:5, exhorting his son in the Gospel, uses the word *"commandment"* and the meaning of the word is <u>mandate</u> or calling. *"The end of the <u>commandment</u> is charity out of a pure heart."* Because we love righteousness, being foundational, we hate iniquity. Because we love God and his plan and because we *"fear, lest, a promise being left us of entering into his rest, any of you should seem to come short of it"* (Hebrews 4:1). Thus, we continue as faithful partakers of the "pathway of charity," which is the heart of the "doctrine of eternal judgment." To wit:

Judgment: The format for restitution. It is our calling, and it is our course. It has two ends. One is that which continues into eternity; <u>eternal</u> life, even immortality. We fervently desire that blessed estate, being a oneness with God, in our Lord and Savior Jesus Christ (at-one-ment). The other end is <u>eternal</u> damnation. Thus, we understand the doctrine of *"eternal judgment"*: Two ends, two manifestations of purification, two voices, twofold in the overview of man's six-thousand-year tenure; two directions on this path of eternal judgment. Again, God loves his creatures and his creation; above all, he loves his son Jesus Christ. We love him and we love his judgment in our own lives, which is unto life eternal. As a similitude, "salt" is judgment. If the salt has savor, it is judgment unto eternal life. Contrariwise, an estate of "judgment unto eternal death" is *"good for nothing."* Salt having no savor is *"good for nothing, but to be cast out, and to be trodden under foot of men"* (Matthew 5:13). <u>The pathway of charity (love) is our walk/path, and it is the pith and marrow of the doctrine of eternal judgment. Love is foundational toward the judgment of all things.</u>

Having discussed love and judgment and their integration into one purpose/accomplishment, let us go to a "similitude" that will better complete the vision. From the beginning of God's dealing with mankind, he has often elected to show his will and plan by "similitudes." Scripture is replete with examples. A connected Scripture: Solomon stated in Proverbs 25:2, *"It is the glory of God to conceal a thing: but the honour of kings is to search out a matter."*

Jacob's Ladder: We have heard it said: Don't stop with the messenger, lest you fall short of a full embrace of the message. So, it is with personal sacrifice. Pain and suffering may be a sort of messenger, but the great and overriding sacrifice is Christ: <u>his</u> pain and suffering and <u>his</u> example. As such, <u>Jesus is the Door</u>. The Door which makes the ascension to salvation possible; a quickening from dead to living, then growing to the likeness of Christ. <u>Jesus is the message</u>. We are messengers, in the sense of being a visible senior disciple and ambassador.

Jesus told Nathanael, *"Hereafter ye shall see heaven open, and the angels of God ascending and descending upon the Son of man"* (John 1:51). This exactly reflects the vision of <u>Jacob's ladder</u>, *"And he dreamed, and behold a ladder set up on the earth, and the top of it reached to heaven: and behold the angels of God ascending and descending on it."* He confessed later, *"This is none other but the house of God, and this is the gate of heaven"* (Genesis 28:12, 17). Jesus is the door and he is the gate. John 10:1 states, *"Verily, verily, I say unto you, He that entereth not by the door into the sheepfold, but climbeth up some other way, the same is a thief and a robber." Ascending* and *climbeth* are the same word. He is the ladder because doors, plural, become a ladder. (A chain of doorposts and lintels, or, better said, a vertical stack of doorposts and lintels, would indeed become a ladder. This requires no stretch of the imagination.)

"Except a corn of wheat fall into the ground and die, it abideth alone: but if it die, it bringeth forth much fruit" (John 12:24). Jesus' blood is God's very signature on the lintel and doorpost of that *"corn of wheat."* The first of 144,000. It is noteworthy that only one door of the ladder portrayed has a threshold and that is the bottom or foundational door. Jesus tasted death for all, and was buried, *"and declared to be the Son of God with power, according to the spirit of holiness, by the resurrection from the dead"* (Romans 1:4). The fact is that Jesus, and him crucified, is our heavenly connection and the very path of salvation. This is our ascent to the spiritual things of God. He is our mediator and the avenue of angelic administration.

Collectivewise, we can see the *"ladder"* representing the saving heavenly connection, the binding of Satan, the eventual judgment, and the restitution of all things. A like similitude: <u>It is the "chain" that will bind Satan</u> (Revelation 20:1). It is our godly desire that he will elect us to be a link in that chain, and one of the "door" reflections; so, being that *"an entrance shall be ministered unto you abundantly into the everlasting kingdom of our Lord and Saviour Jesus Christ"* (2 Peter 1:11). Jesus is our door. According to his determination and provision of abundant grace, we hope for graduation to ladder/chain exemplary status. That would be: The very elect, the Bride of Christ. The end point calling of the very elect is not only to die daily; the calling is to die literally, as martyrs. That may not happen, but there is a willingness, even desire, if the occasion requires.

The shed blood of Jesus Christ was the greatest judgment of evil in the annals of mankind. It always will be. The shed blood of 144,000 chosen elect is also a great judgment factor. That number, of which the remnant is soon to be complete, will be the "second witness" toward God's judgment of evil in the heavens and in the earth.

Rest assured, God's righteous judgment will extract the equivalent shed blood of *"the vine of the earth."* On that point, be encouraged with the following noteworthy *"hard to be understood"* but precious similitude:

1,600 Furlongs: *"And the angel thrust in his sickle into the earth, and gathered the vine of the earth, and cast it into the great winepress of the wrath of God. And the winepress was trodden without the city, and blood came out of the winepress, even unto the horse bridles, by the space of a thousand and six hundred furlongs"* (Revelation 14:19, 20).

This passage has special meaning for those who desire understanding relating to the High Calling; that is, the Bride, the Very Elect, the Man Child, the 144,000.

One thousand six hundred furlongs is the measure of blood that results from God's wrath on the vine of the earth. It is the concluding judgment on six thousand years of evil perpetuated by the unrighteous line, the seed of the serpent, and the world. Revelation 18:24 states, *"And in her was found the blood of prophets, and of saints, and of all that were slain upon the earth."*

The blood depicted by the 1,600 furlongs equates to the shed blood of the 144,000 Saints. That insight rest on a faith in God's divine will and his divine justice. God does not merely measure blood quantities. He is declaring, by this depiction, the principle of righteous judgment and justice. We are looking at the atonement and the beginning of the thousand-year restitution of all things. *"Whom the heaven must receive until the times of restitution of all things, which God hath spoken by the mouth of all his holy prophets since the world began"* (Acts 3:21).

What we are reaching toward in this writing is the righteous line of judgment laid across the whole of the matter. To wit: Jesus, and then the 144,000, constitutes the first and second witnesses that declare God's justice and the judgment of all things.

Pertaining expressly to the judgment of the heavenly rank: *"Yea, the heavens are not clean in his sight"* (Job 15:15). Paul said, *"Know ye not that we shall judge angels?"* (1 Corinthians 6:3).

Isaiah 28:17 states, *"Judgment also will I lay to the line, and righteousness to the plummet."* God's final manifest righteousness is as the plumbline laid over in death. The deaths of the saints become the line of judgment in the ultimate or final sense. *"Righteousness and judgment are the habitation of his throne"* (Psalms 97:2). Again, *"Judgment also will I lay to the line, and righteousness to the plummet."* Righteous lives are a living judgment factor (height standing/horse bridles), but, if given sacrificially, that is prone or laid over in martyrdom, the measure of the 144,000 is 1,600 furlongs. It concludes all judgment, *"Precious in the sight of the Lord is the death of his saints"* (Psalms 116:15). We'll do the arithmetic later.

The righteous line of the Old Testament era is fulfilled in the Firstborn of the New Testament. Jesus is the *"seed,"* singular (Galatians 3:16), while the *"church of the firstborn"* (Hebrews 12:23) denotes the plural part.

An additional comment on the line (judgment) and the plummet (righteousness), and the birthright (double portion) and the blessing (transfer of heritage). The reason being, it is the heart and calling of the Saints.

Regarding the New Testament equivalent of birthright and blessing: The birthright is that double portion; *"Even the spirit of truth . . . for he dwelleth with you, and shall be in you"* (John 14:17). Also, *"Christ in you, the hope of glory"* (Colossians 1:27). We are not alone; we have Jesus with and in us, and, thus, we are a twofold witness. Relating to the judgment factor: *"It is also written in your law, that the testimony of two men is true. I am one that bear witness of myself, and the Father that sent me beareth witness of me"* (John 8:17, 18). This is a double portion in the most extraordinary manner. *"Judgment . . . to the line."*

The blessing is the imputing of righteousness. In 2 Corinthians 5:21, it states, *"For he hath made him to be sin for us, who knew no sin; that we might be made the righteousness of God in him."* Or, *"righteousness to the plummet."*

The overcomer reflects God's righteousness-and-judgment which is the plummet-and-line of God in the earth (Isaiah 28:17). This understanding reflects our individual and collective mandate, so that God cleanses heaven and earth. Going forward, entering into the Lord's Day, there will be 144,000 Jews, terrestrials, posi-tioned to implement God's will on the earth. Concurrently, there will be 144,000 very elect, Bride celestials, positioned to judge and cast out evil from the realm of heaven. This judgment is not accomplished by over-comers pointing a finger of accusation. It is accomplished when God's enemies point the finger of accusa-tion, and proceed to kill the righteous; and that being altogether without justification.

The 144,000 Bride members are God's very elect chosen for that status: Bride of Christ. They represent the high-water mark, so to speak, of the judgment of all things heavenly and earthly. The offering of their per-fected sacrifice answers/defeats all accusations of the enemy; thus, judging the enemy. Jesus accomplished this perfectly on the cross. He was the first and the primary witness. The very elect will be the second witness which concludes the six-thousand-year era. Stephen was such a second witness that concluded the Jew's four-hundred-ninety-year era. Again: The first observance of an overcomer is their upright, circumspect walk before God and man. With time, the sacrificial part becomes more evident. Ultimately, they suffer mar-tyrdom at the hands of God's enemies. If this is at the hands of those possessed of devils, then such a sacrifice will certainly judge man and demon.

An upright, exemplary person fulfills the measure of the horse's bridle. That similitude reflects the righ-teous overcomer. As that precious life is laid down in martyrdom, we see another measure portrayed. What is that measure? Repeat: If the measure of the overcomers was the horses' bridle, then what would be the mea-sure of their collective sacrificed lives laid down in martyrdom? The answer is 1,600 furlongs; 144,000 times the measure of the door. Remember, the door is the passage or entry into Grace and that door is Christ. This similitude reflects God's measure of abundant Grace in the life of the 144,000 overcomers. That constitutes, or equates, to a judgment factor on earth.

While this section amplifies on a specified very elect, there is no marginalizing of the multiplied millions of lives lived and graduated to eternal life. All, terrestrials and celestials, are, in Jesus' example, being judg-ment factors. They are forever, perfect citizens of the New Heaven and New Earth.

Let us carry the similitude forward and do the math: Jesus is the Door. If we look at a door's height, prone, as if sacrificed, or laid down; then what would 144,000 doors measure? What would be the measure of that line of judgment, laid by God across the earth? To wit: Jesus and the 144,000 second witness? Do the math:

The late thirteenth century saw the furlong change from 600 old feet to 660 new feet. At the time of John's writing, approximately AD 100, the furlong was the measure of the best recognized stadium track, approxi-mately 625 feet. Let us just simplify the matter of distance and say, according to today's measure, it would be 660 feet/furlong x 1,600 furlongs = 1,056,000 feet (200 miles). Divided by 144,000 = 7.33' or 7' 4". Using the more probable figure of 625 feet/furlong x 1,600 furlongs = 1,000,000 feet. Divided by 144,000 = 6' 11". These figures approximate the measurement of a typical door frame height. 6' 11" to 7' 4".

The sacrificed blood of the pure, perfected, and innocent is the basis and "justification factor" in the con-clusion of this end-time judgment plan. That is, 144,000 lives given, being dead to this passing first heaven and first earth. This numerical similitude reflects how exacting God is, and how precious the Saints are in his sight and in the heart of our Lord Jesus Christ. It reflects the "Spirit" of the Plan and God's "Intent." It is "His Word" and that is our "Vision." God is Love and our calling is to love God, love one another, and love God's plan as it exists in the Lord Jesus.

This book, for its many words, is a pale shadow of the fathomless and grand magnitude of God's Eternal Plan. He is our Father. His Christ is our Savior. We are Family and we are loved.

Postscript

THIS WRITING PRESENTS THE scenario of a Church Body of which Christ is the head. It will be unified, evidently put forth for public scrutiny, accountable, transparent, and harmless. A mystery but not mystical, strong but sacrificial and servantlike. Such an occurrence is unthinkable in the light of carnal reasonings and the natural reckoning of things possible. This present world accelerates toward cancel culture, secularism, chaos, and anti-Christianity. So, you ask, *"Where is the house that ye build unto me? and where is the place of my rest"* (Isaiah 66:1)? Believers answer: The cry will go forth, *"Come out of her, my people"* (Revelation 18:4). God's people will come together. God will have a people of which he is the head. Christ's voice and example will be manifest and declared to this end generation. This is our faith; the same *"faith which was once delivered unto the saints"* (Jude 3).

www.ingramcontent.com/pod-product-compliance
Lightning Source LLC
Chambersburg PA
CBHW081233090426
42738CB00016B/3289